TEACH YOUR
DOG
NEW TRICKS

TEACH YOUR
DOG
NEW TRICKS

Step-by-Step Instructions for Novice, Intermediate, and Advanced Tricks

Hannah Richter

ROCKRIDGE
PRESS

For general information on our other products and services or to obtain technical support, please contact our Customer Care Department within the U.S. at (866) 744-2665, or outside the U.S. at (510) 253-0500.

Rockridge Press publishes its books in a variety of electronic and print formats. Some content that appears in print may not be available in electronic books, and vice versa.

Interior and Cover Designer: Lindsey Dekker
Photo Art Director/Art Manager: Michael Hardgrove
Editor: Arturo Conde
Production Editor: Ashley Polikoff
Custom Illustrations © 2020 Kate Francis
Interior art used under license from © iStockphoto.com & Shutterstock.com
Author photo credit: Turner Rouse, Jr.

ISBN: Print 978-1-64739-267-3 | eBook 978-1-64739-268-0
R0

*This book is for my mom, Enid Richter,
who gave me my love of dogs.*

CONTENTS

INTRODUCTION

No matter their age or size, all dogs can learn new tricks! Whether you want your dog to learn a classic move like a Roll Over (see page 44) or a more advanced trick like Cross Your Paws (see page 147), this guide will show you how to teach new tricks to your dog in detailed, easy-to-follow steps.

Teaching your dog new tricks has many benefits, including strengthening the bond between you and your pet. Training helps you develop a language together. As you and your dog learn to read each other's body language, your relationship becomes closer and you start to understand each other on a deeper level. When you communicate clearly, your dog learns to trust you and feels more confident working with you.

Tricks training also has many physical and mental health benefits. For example, it's an engaging way to develop and strengthen your dog's muscles. Sit Pretty (see page 50) requires a dog to use their core, which means your dog may need to develop that core strength before mastering the trick. Having a strong core improves a dog's overall balance and athletic ability, and it helps protect their spine from injury. Other tricks, such as a Bow (see page 47), help stretch your dog's muscles, which promotes overall flexibility and circulation.

Many dog parents focus on working out their dog's physical energy, but they often forget about burning mental energy. Spending time exercising your dog's mind through tricks training helps them develop better learning skills, communication, and manners. When your dog spends time burning mental energy, you will find that they are more relaxed and satisfied when you need to take your focus elsewhere. You will be surprised at how tired your dog will be after a tricks training session!

The Anatomy of a Dog Trick

The training process for learning new tricks can be broken down into three basic parts. Each new behavior is made up of a cue, an action, and a reward.

- A cue is a visual or verbal signal that prompts your dog to perform a specific behavior. An example of a cue would be saying the word "sit" to signal your dog to sit down.

- An action is the behavior you are prompting your dog to do. For example, the action of a Sit is the motion of your dog getting into a sit position. The moment your dog's rear is on the ground, you mark your dog as correct by using a marker—either a clicker or a marker word (see page 6).

- After you mark your dog as correct, you reward them with a treat to reinforce their behavior.

By working in this way, you are able to establish a fun and gentle method of learning with your dog. Keep in mind that consistency, repetition, and timing are fundamental pillars for all types of learning.

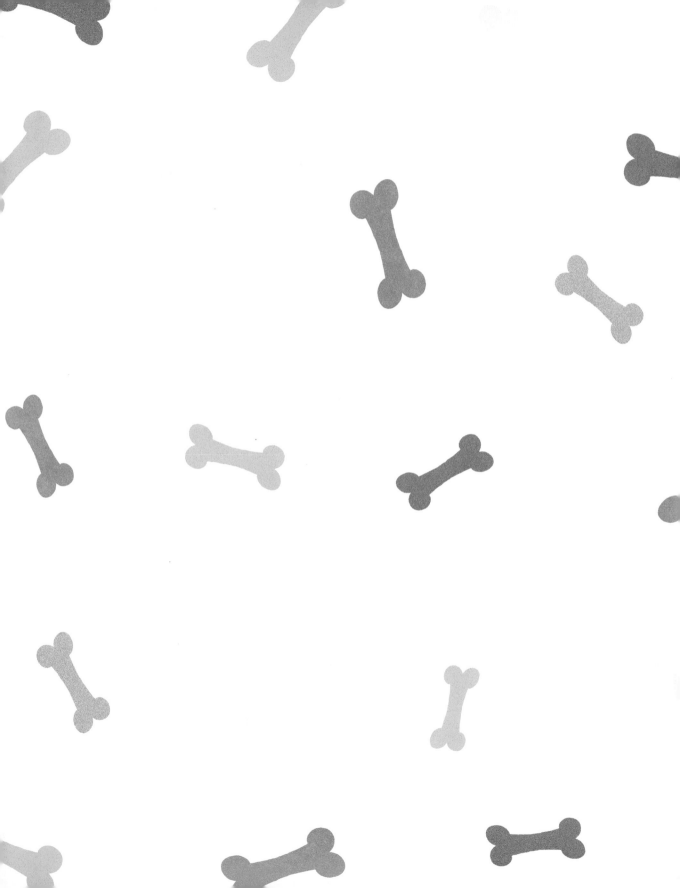

CHAPTER 1

Understanding Basic Training Principles

Here's a dog training secret: The best way to set your dog up for success is to commit to training them with patience, kindness, and encouragement. This chapter will help you be the best teacher you can be for your dog.

What Kind of Teacher Do You Want to Be?

Write out the qualities you have appreciated in your favorite teachers, such as enthusiasm, patience, and dedication. Can you incorporate those same qualities into training sessions with your dog? When you create a positive and rewarding learning environment, you are setting yourself and your dog up for success.

As you work through this book, remember that one of the most effective methods for learning something new is to break a task or lesson down into essential steps. In dog training, each trick is made up of a chain of several smaller behaviors. This chaining, or stringing multiple behaviors together, makes it possible to learn complex tricks.

In chapter 7 (see page 133), for instance, Blanket Roll Up—where the dog rolls up in a blanket—is made up of three individual behaviors that are chained together: Down, Grab It, and Roll Over. You'll need to make sure your dog can perform all three behaviors separately before you can start to string them together. Because each step must be learned individually, it can take months to master a complex trick.

How You Should Use This Book

Before beginning any new tricks, be sure to check with your vet if you have any concerns about your dog's physical health. It's important not to over-work your dog and to avoid any exercises that put a lot of pressure on your dog's major joints. This is especially important when working with young puppies, elderly dogs, or dogs with preexisting medical conditions.

Start at the front of the book and work through to the end. The tricks in chapters 2 (see page 13) and 3 (see page 35) will help you—and are at times necessary—when learning more advanced tricks. Learning these tricks first sets a strong foundation for the future. Always work through each step of the instructions in the order listed. Skipping steps could cause your dog to learn the trick incorrectly or could cause injury.

Pick three or four tricks to focus on in each practice session. Work on each exercise daily until your dog has the behavior on cue. Once you have those down, you can pick a new group of tricks. Learning takes time, so remember to be patient and work at a speed that keeps your dog engaged and motivated. Most importantly, have fun! Tricks are rewarding activities that bring joy and smiles to humans and dogs alike.

THREE D'S OF TRAINING

When your dog becomes more consistent with cues, you can challenge their behavior by adding distance, distraction, and duration. Trainers commonly refer to these as the three D's. Working with one at a time adds difficulty to each trick. Let's review how each will help your dog develop their skill levels.

Distance: Adding distance means that you are increasing the space between you and your dog. For example, if you add distance to a Sit Stay, work on increasing the number of steps you take away from your dog as they perform the trick.

Distraction: Adding distraction means that you are working around or adding something in the environment that may take your dog's focus away from the behavior. Common distractions include other dogs, sounds, and throwing treats.

Duration: Adding on duration means that you are increasing the amount of time your dog is required to hold the position.

Setting Expectations

Making realistic goals for you and your dog keeps training fun and helps you both feel successful. Just like people, dogs learn at different paces. Although each trick in the book lists an estimated learning time, dogs have different personalities, bodies, and genetics, so real learning times will vary. Being patient and keeping a positive attitude is crucial for mastering new tricks. You and your dog are capable of learning any of the tricks in this book with repetition and time—and the right expectations!

Training in the morning and early evening works the best for most dogs because they are hungry and motivated to work for their food. If you have a busy work schedule, set time aside for a short session before you leave in the morning and another in the evening when you get home. Doing so will also help keep your dog relaxed throughout the day. If your schedule is more flexible, shoot for three training sessions that last between 10 and 15 minutes each day. Short sessions are more effective than long ones.

You can train your dog in any room that has enough space for both of you to move around comfortably. Living rooms and bedrooms tend to work well. Once your dog responds consistently to cues in the home, practice in different environments, such as outside or a space with other dogs.

Overworking your dog can leave a negative impression on them. Dogs often show that they are frustrated with a calming signal, such as shaking off, lip licking, excessive sniffing, scratching, and excessive drooling. If you notice that your dog is stressed, take a play break or practice a few behaviors that they know well. If your dog is having trouble with a trick, break it down into even smaller pieces. Avoid becoming tense or frustrated because your dog will pick up on that energy and may associate it with the exercise. Instead, keep a cheery tone and praise and reward them to stay motivated. If your dog doesn't perform the behavior correctly, reset and try again. Be your dog's biggest cheerleader. Always try to end your session on a positive note so that you both leave feeling satisfied and accomplished.

Consistency pays off. You will see the most progress by working daily with your dog, but sometimes it just isn't doable. If you skip a day or two of practice, your dog will likely remember the work you have done. However, if you skip several weeks or months, you may need to go back a few steps when you have your next session. If you're having trouble, use a treat to lure your dog into the behavior, reminding them what you are cueing. Reward with a treat for a few repetitions and then try again.

Why We Only Use Positive Reinforcement

Imagine that every time you went to class, you were praised and given a big paycheck. Pretty soon, you would really look forward to going to school. This is how you want your dog to feel about training. Instead of money, you will use treats, toys, and other rewards as "payment" for your dog. Experts say that positive reinforcement is the most effective way to train, and this book advocates for positive reinforcement in all of its exercises.

Positive reinforcement is a teaching method that rewards your dog after they offer the correct response. This increases the likelihood of your dog remembering and offering that behavior again. When you use rewards to reinforce your dog, you develop a way to tell your dog when you like how they are acting. Dogs are very good at learning the consequences of their actions. For example, if you positively reinforce a Sit a lot, your dog will start to offer Sit frequently. Your dog will learn that by responding to your cues and offering the correct behaviors, they will get rewarded.

Do *not*, under any circumstance, use physical manipulation, force, yelling, or any other type of punitive behavior on your dog. Doing so will make your dog fear you and the training. You want your dog to feel confident and successful in their training sessions, not scared. If your dog doesn't offer the desired behavior, simply do not reward them, reset, and try again. Focus on rewarding the behaviors you like versus correcting the behaviors that do not meet expectations.

The tricks in this guide include troubleshooting tips to help you adjust the training when your dog is not behaving as expected. As a general tip, try working at a slower pace and review the step-by-step instructions. This can really help clarify behavior for your dog.

Remember to be consistent and reward the small victories. Let's take a look at some of the methods you can use to teach using positive reinforcement.

Luring. When you begin teaching a new trick to your dog, it is helpful to use a training method called "lure and reward." This means that you use a treat to lure, or guide, your dog as you teach them new behaviors.

Shaping. Another way you can teach your dog is by shaping a behavior, or rewarding successive approximations until you reach your end goal. An example of this is rewarding any movement your dog makes toward the floor when working on a Down cue. Over several training sessions, increase the criteria by only rewarding your dog when they move even closer to the ground.

Capturing. You can also teach your dog by using capturing, a training method in which you wait for the dog to offer the behavior on their own and then you mark and reward them. An example of capturing would be marking and rewarding your dog when you notice them in a Bow position naturally, such as after waking up from a nap.

Why We Use Clickers and Marker Words

You can tricks train anywhere with your dog. All you need is your dog and some treats—and a clicker if you want!

A clicker is a small handheld button that makes a *click* sound when you press it. Trainers use the clicker to let dogs know the exact moment when they are behaving correctly. After the click, dogs are rewarded with a treat. One click always predicts one treat. Your dog will learn to remember what they were doing when they hear the click, which means the timing of the click is crucial. When teaching a dog to Sit, for instance, you click the moment their rear touches the ground. The click and the treat reinforce the Sit position. You need to practice to get the timing right.

If you prefer not to use a clicker, use a marker word. A marker word functions in the same way as a clicker. Use a short, easily recognizable word like "Good" or "Yes" to mark the moment your dog behaves correctly. Just like with clicker training, reward one treat per every marker word.

This exercise teaches your dog the sound of the clicker. Repeating these steps will get your dog to love the click as it will teach them to expect a treat when they hear the sound of the clicker:

1. Press the button on the clicker.
2. Give your dog a treat.

After you charge the clicker, use the clicker to mark behaviors in your training sessions. When your dog consistently performs a behavior, fade the clicker out. The clicker is most effective when used in the beginning stages of teaching a new trick. Use a marker word when you don't have a clicker and when working to fade the click out.

Transitioning to Visual and Verbal Cues

As your training becomes more advanced, you will want to guide your dog's behavior with different types of cues. You can cue your dog by using visual and verbal cues.

The first step to shaping a visual or verbal cue is fading out the lure. To do so, you need to get your dog to rely less on seeing treats up front. First, you must teach them that rewards can come from places other than your cue hand. Then you transition to a visual cue and verbal cue. After teaching you the primary trick steps, most tricks in this book then explain how to transition away from the lure, how to add a visual cue, and how to add a verbal cue.

VISUAL CUES

A visual cue is a hand, foot, or body gesture that prompts your dog to perform an action. Your dog is naturally fantastic at reading body language. Because of their keen sense of movement, it is usually most effective to teach your dog the visual cue first before installing a verbal cue. Once the dog is able to offer the behavior consistently with a visual cue, you add the verbal cue. In this book, you'll use the following visual cues.

Are You Tired? (Chin Down): Touch the back of your fingers to your chin

Arm Hoop Jumps: Holding arms out to your side in a ring shape

Back Up: Beep, Beep: Open, flat palm with fingertips pointing downward, making a pushing motion

Belly Up: Open your palm facing up, flip over your hand for cue

Blanket Roll Up: Pointing to a towel or blanket with the verbal cue "Roll Up"

Bow: Curtsy or bow

Clean Up: Put Your Toys Away: Pointing to a toy with the verbal cue "Clean Up"

Contact: Back Legs On: Point to an object with the verbal cue "Contact"

Cover Your Eyes: Hand near your nose

Crawl: Two fingers moving along the ground

Dog Circles You: A slight lean to your right and left side

Down: Open, flat palm facing down, moving downward

Figure Eight: Standing with legs apart with one knee slightly bent

Get It: Presenting an object with the verbal cue "Get it"

Get Your Leash: Pointing to a leash with the verbal cue "Get Your Leash"

Go to Bed: Point to your dog's bed

Heel: Index finger pointing down at side

High-Five: Flat, open palm with fingertips pointing toward the ceiling

High-Ten: Two flat, open palms with fingertips pointing toward the ceiling

Hug: Kneeling with hands reaching toward your dog

Jump Over Arms: Kneeling with an arm out to the side

Jump Over Legs: Finger pointing over your legs

Leg Weaves Walking: Stepping with one leg forward and pointing near one side

Monkey: Holding forearm up near dog and parallel to the ground with verbal cue "Monkey"

Nod Yes: Nod your head

Paw: Cupped palm facing up with fingers touching

Paw to Foot: Holding one foot out

Perch: Pointing to an object with the verbal cue "Perch"

Post: Standing with legs slightly apart, one finger pointed down

Quiet: Finger to lips as if saying "Shh"

Rest: Chin on Lap: One hand on your lap

Roll Over: Point your index finger in front of yourself and draw a small circle

Sit: Open, flat palm facing up, moving slightly upward

Sit Pretty: Fist moving up

Snoot: Index finger and thumb touching with other fingers spread out, like an okay sign

Speak: Thumb touching fingertips like a duckbill, opening and closing

Spin: Pointing index finger toward the ground and moving in a small circle

Stand: Open, flat palm facing up with slightly curled fingertips, moving in toward yourself (like opening a drawer)

Stay: Pointing index finger as if showing the number one

Touch: Palm facing up, slightly cupped, moving toward paw

Up: All Four Paws On: Tap the object with your hand twice

Up Tall: Hand showing two fingers, like the "number-two" sign

Watch: Holding a hand near your collarbone or face

Wave: Wave your hand

A verbal cue is a word or sound that prompts the dog to perform an action. When you add a verbal cue to a behavior, it is important that you only say the cue word one time so that your dog learns to respond promptly to the cue. If you say the word over and over again, your dog will never learn what you are asking of them. If someone repeated the word "dog" in a foreign language over and over again to you, the meaning wouldn't become clear just because the word was repeated.

This is why you teach your dog the definition of the word with a lure before the visual and verbal cues. Then you can label the behavior with a word that you will say only once. Do not say the verbal cue at the same time as you show the visual cue because your dog will block one cue out.

In this guide, you will use the following verbal cues:

- Are You Tired?
- Beep, Beep
- Bow
- Catch
- Circle
- Clean Up
- Contact
- Crawl
- Down
- Drop It
- Eight
- Find It
- Foot
- Get It
- Get Your Leash
- Heel
- High-Five
- High-Ten
- Hoop

- How Was Your Dinner?
- Hug
- Jump
- Leave It
- Left
- Monkey
- Nod
- Okay
- Paw
- Perch
- Post
- Quiet
- Rest
- Right
- Roll Over
- Roll Up
- Shake
- Sit
- Sit Pretty

- Snoot
- Speak
- Stand
- Stay
- Tap
- Through
- Touch
- Watch
- Wave
- Where's Mommy/Daddy?

Why Your Dog Needs to Be Rewarded

Rewards make it possible for you to communicate with your dog that they are correct. They also keep your dog motivated and determined to succeed. In dog training, you use food to tell your dog that they have done a good job, which makes them have a positive association with those behaviors. Treats motivate your dog to want to figure out what behavior you are asking for. Each time you reward your dog for a specific behavior, you are reinforcing that behavior. The more a behavior is reinforced, the more likely your dog is to offer it again.

When you use food to reward your dog, you must break your treats into tiny pieces. Each reward should be about the size of a pea or smaller. Tiny treats allow you to get in a lot of repetitions without your dog getting too full. You need to use treats that your dog absolutely loves. Work with at least three different treats so that you have options if your dog loses interest in one. If your dog seems to be unmotivated or distracted, switch to a higher value treat, such as boiled chicken or string cheese—something your dog loves but doesn't normally get. Doing so will make your dog want to work for the food. Some dogs prefer to be rewarded with a toy. If this is the case, let your dog play tug or fetch for each correct response.

Spend time learning which treats your dog prefers to work for. Write out a treat scale by listing your dog's favorite treat at number 10 and a treat they like, but that they get often, at number 1. Start to train with a lower value treat so that you have higher value treats to use if your dog becomes unfocused. Here's an example list:

1. Kibble
2. Carrots
3. Wellness Core Beef Jerky Bites
4. Stella and Chewy's Meal Mixers or Dinner Patties
5. Freeze-dried chicken breast
6. Freeze-dried beef liver
7. Freeze-dried chicken hearts
8. Freeze-dried beef hearts
9. Cheese
10. Chicken

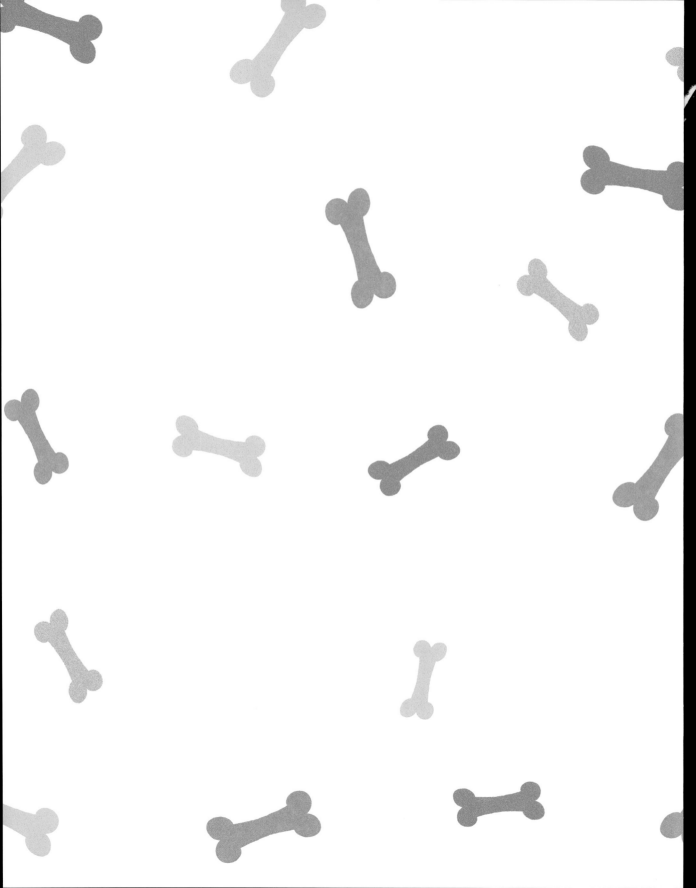

CHAPTER 2

Master the Basics

Before you teach your dog tricks, they need to know a few basic cues. These behaviors in this chapter serve as the foundation for the other tricks in this guide. This foundation is the most important part of tricks training, so spend time working these behaviors before you continue on.

Tricks can be broken down into several smaller behaviors that are chained together. This means you and your dog need to practice a handful of behaviors before you can begin stringing them together into more complex tricks. For example, a Crawl (see page 90) is made up of a Down cue followed by the forward crawling motion. If your dog has never learned a Down cue, learning a Crawl will be impossible.

Even if you have previously worked on these cues, go through each trick and start to add more challenges, such as the three D's (see page 3). As your training progresses, return to the behaviors in this chapter at the start of your training sessions as a way to check in with your pup and get them ready to learn.

Sit

Verbal Cue
Sit

Visual Cue
Open, flat palm
facing down,
moving downward

Sit is without a doubt the most popular trick. It is the foundation of many tricks and is a behavior that you can use to prevent your dog from practicing bad habits, such as jumping up on people or counters. When your dog is sitting, it is impossible for them to jump up. Try to predict when your dog will jump and ask them to sit instead. Cue your dog to offer a Sit before you give them any reward, such as throwing a ball, giving them dinner, letting them out of the yard, opening the front door, etc. You want your dog to think that sitting is a really cool trick that always gets rewarded highly.

How Long Will It Take? 10 repetitions two times per day for two weeks for each visual and verbal cue

1. Pinch a treat between your thumb and fingertips.

2. Hold a treat close to your dog's nose.

3. Slowly lift up and slightly back between the dog's ears and over their head. Their chin and nose will follow the treat up and their rear will go down like a seesaw.

4. Mark your dog as correct with your clicker or marker word the moment their bottom touches the floor and they sit.

5. Reward with a yummy treat.

NEED HELP?

If your dog isn't following the treat, allow your dog to gently lick or nibble on the treat before moving your hand. Try to keep the treat at nose level to prevent jumping.

If your dog jumps, pull the treat away and let them try again.

When they offer a Sit, mark them as correct and reward.

If your dog gets up, try to take the treat away for a split second without your dog getting up and then reward them. This comes in handy when extending duration (see page 17).

You want to be faster than your dog so that you catch them with the reward before they get up.

HOW TO WORK THE TREAT OUT OF YOUR CUE HAND

1. Pinch a treat between your thumb and fingertips in both hands.

2. Place your left hand behind your back.

3. Lure your dog to Sit with your right hand.

4. Mark your dog as correct when their rear touches the ground.

5. Reward with a treat from your left hand.

6. Take the treats out of your right hand. Pretend to have a treat in your right hand and ask for Sit again.

7. Mark when they Sit and reward from your left hand.

8. Repeat with your left hand giving the cue and your right hand behind your back.

HOW TO ADD A VISUAL CUE

1. Show your dog an open, flat palm facing up, moving slightly upward, then lure them into the Sit using a treat to remind them of the behavior.

2. Mark when your dog's rear touches the ground.

3. Reward with a treat.

4. When your dog begins to respond to the visual cue consistently, start to add a pause after you show your dog the visual cue to give them time to offer the correct behavior before you use the treat.

5. Mark your dog as correct when your dog Sits and reward with a treat.

HOW TO ADD A VERBAL CUE

1. Say the verbal cue "Sit" one time just before showing the visual cue to your dog.

2. Mark when your dog Sits.

3. Reward with a treat.

4. When your dog begins to respond to the verbal cue consistently, start to add a pause after you say the verbal cue to give your dog time to offer the correct behavior.

5. When your dog begins to respond consistently to the cues, you can pick either the verbal or visual cue to ask them for a Sit.

1. Use a treat to lure your dog into the Sit position.

2. Mark them as correct when they Sit and give them a treat.

3. Take the treat quickly away and then give it back after a moment.

4. At first your dog will need rapid treating. I recommend quickly flicking your wrist away and then bringing it back.

5. Start to increase the time in between treats. Be sure to vary the intervals (e.g., 1, 4, 2, 7, and 3 seconds) so that your dog cannot guess how long you are going to ask them to hold the position.

6. When you are ready to release them, say "Okay" and toss a treat. When your dog gets up, mark and reward them as correct. Be sure to say "Okay" before you toss the treat so that your dog learns to respond to your verbal cue, not the treat toss.

Down

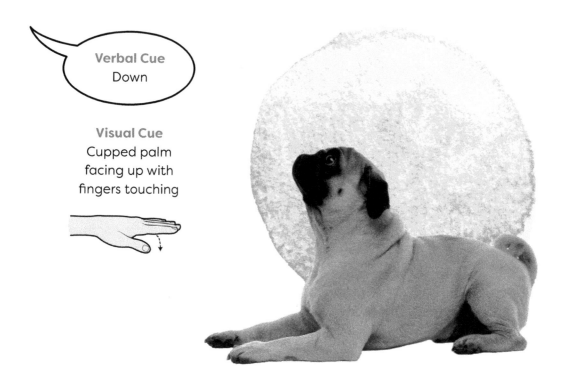

Verbal Cue
Down

Visual Cue
Cupped palm
facing up with
fingers touching

Did you know that being in a down position naturally relaxes your dog? Having a solid Down is endlessly useful for manners and tricks skills. Down is the foundation for many behaviors such as Roll Over (see page 44) and Crawl (see page 90). You can also use this cue when you want your dog to chill out. Having a solid Down cue means that you can travel with your dog without feeling anxious about their behavior.

How Long Will It Take? 10 repetitions two times per day for three weeks for each visual and verbal cue

1. Pinch a treat between your thumb and fingertips, and turn your palm to face down.

2. Hold a treat close to your dog's nose or allow your dog to gently lick or nibble on the treat.

3. Slowly bring the treat toward the ground, just between their front paws and slightly in.

4. When their belly and all four legs are touching the ground, mark them as correct with your clicker or marker word and reward with a treat.

NEED HELP?

Reward your dog for any movement toward the ground. As they get more comfortable and confident with the exercise, you can change the criteria and ask them to move down little by little until they reach the floor.

Because each dog is built differently, you'll need to lure your dog in the way that works best for them. As they get more comfortable, they will reach the Down position.

Some dogs respond better when you move the treat slightly out instead of back. Try both and see which works for you and your dog.

HOW TO WORK THE TREAT OUT OF YOUR CUE HAND

1. Pinch a treat between your thumb and fingertips in both hands.

2. Place your left hand behind your back.

3. Lure your dog to go Down with your right hand.

4. Mark your dog as correct when they go Down.

5. Reward with a treat from your left hand.

6. Take the treats out of your right hand. Pretend to have a treat in your right hand and ask for Down again.

7. Mark when they go Down and reward from your left hand.

8. Repeat with your left hand giving the cue and your right hand behind your back.

HOW TO ADD A VISUAL CUE

1. Show your dog an open, flat palm facing down, moving downward, then lure them into the Down using a treat to remind them of the behavior.

2. Mark when your dog lies down.

3. Reward with a treat.

4. When your dog begins to respond to the visual cue consistently, start to add a pause after you show your dog the visual cue to give them time to offer the correct behavior.

5. Mark your dog as correct when your dog lies down and reward with a treat.

HOW TO ADD A VERBAL CUE

1. Say the verbal cue "Down" one time just before showing the visual cue to your dog.

2. Mark when your dog lies down.

3. Reward with a treat.

4. When your dog begins to respond to the verbal cue consistently, start to add a pause after you say the verbal cue to give your dog time to offer the correct behavior.

5. When your dog begins to respond consistently to the cues, you can pick either the verbal or visual cue to ask them for a Down.

1. Use a treat to lure your dog into the Down position.

2. Mark them as correct when they lie down and give them a treat.

3. Take the treat quickly away and then give it back after a moment.

4. At first your dog will need rapid treating. I recommend quickly flicking your wrist away and then bringing it back. Keep the treat in line with the dog's neck to encourage them to stay Down.

5. Start to increase the time in between treats. Be sure to vary the intervals (e.g., 1, 4, 2, 7, and 3 seconds) so that your dog cannot guess how long you are going to ask them to hold the position.

6. When you are ready to release them, say "Okay" and toss a treat. When your dog gets up, mark and reward them as correct. Be sure to say "Okay" before you toss the treat so that your dog learns to respond to your verbal cue, not the treat toss.

Stand

Verbal Cue
Stand

Visual Cue
Open, flat palm
facing up, moving
in toward you (like
opening a drawer)

Once your dog learns Sit and Down, they will start trying to guess what comes next before you even open your mouth or move your hand. To keep them from trying to predict what you will ask for, throw in an occasional Stand to add another option. Stand is also used when you send your dog to the groomer or the vet. A Stand means that your dog is standing still on four paws.

How Long Will It Take? 10 repetitions two times per day for three weeks for each visual and verbal cue

1. Pinch a treat between your thumb and fingers and turn your palm to face up.

2. Hold the treat close to your dog's nose.

3. Slowly pull the treat in toward your body. The action is like pulling a drawer open.

4. When your dog is standing on all four paws, mark them as correct with your clicker or marker word.

5. Reward with a treat.

NEED HELP?

Think of the treat in your hand like a magnet to your dog's nose. Move very slowly and make sure they are following the lure.

HOW TO WORK THE TREAT OUT OF YOUR CUE HAND

1. Pinch a treat between your thumb and fingertips in both hands.

2. Place your left hand behind your back.

3. Lure your dog to Stand with your right hand.

4. Mark your dog as correct when they stand still on all four paws.

5. Reward with a treat from your left hand.

6. Take the treats out of your right hand. Pretend to have a treat in your right hand and ask for Stand again.

7. Mark when they Stand and reward from your left hand.

8. Repeat with your left hand giving the cue and your right hand behind your back.

HOW TO ADD A VISUAL CUE

1. Pretend that you have a treat in your hand and lure your dog to stand to remind them of the behavior.

2. Mark them as correct when they stand.

3. Reward with a treat.

4. With no treats, open up your palm so that your hand is flat with your palm facing up. Cue your dog to stand by moving your hand in toward your body. The movement of the hand is a similar motion to opening up a drawer.

5. Mark your dog as correct when they stand.

6. Reward with a treat.

HOW TO ADD A VERBAL CUE

1. Say the verbal cue "Stand" one time just before showing the visual cue to your dog.

2. Mark when your dog Stands.

3. Reward with a treat.

4. When your dog begins to respond to the verbal cue consistently, start to add a pause after you say the verbal cue to give your dog time to offer the correct behavior.

5. When your dog begins to respond consistently to the cues, you can pick either the verbal or visual cue to ask them for a Stand.

Touch

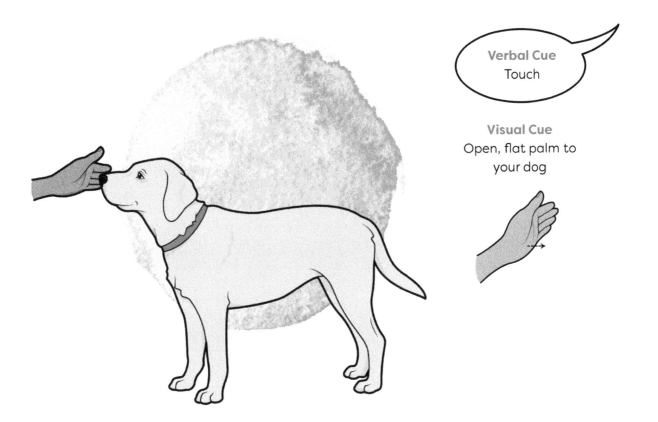

Verbal Cue
Touch

Visual Cue
Open, flat palm to
your dog

A "hand target" is a recall cue that teaches your dog to touch their nose to your hand when you hold it out to them. Short-distance hand targets are used often during tricks training. When you add distance, this behavior will become a Come When Called behavior. Having a solid recall cue is one of the most important behaviors you can teach your dog to keep them safe. Hand targeting is one of my favorite behaviors because it helps me guide my dog easily through space. I love to ask for a hand target before throwing my dogs' toys.

How Long Will It Take? 10 repetitions two times per day for three weeks for each visual and verbal cue

1. Present your palm within six inches of your dog's nose.

2. The moment your dog touches their nose to your hand, mark them as correct with your clicker or marker word.

3. Reward with a treat.

If your dog doesn't respond, try slightly wiggling your fingers, moving your hand a bit through space, or taking your hand away and presenting it again. Rub a small treat on your palm to help attract their nose.

1. Say the verbal cue "Touch" one time just before presenting your palm to your dog.

2. Mark when your dog touches your palm with their nose.

3. Reward with a treat.

4. When your dog responds to the verbal cue consistently, add a pause after you say the verbal cue to give your dog time to offer correct behavior.

5. When your dog begins to respond consistently to the cues, you can pick either the verbal or visual cue to ask them for a Touch.

1. Say the verbal cue "Touch" just before presenting your palm to your dog.

2. Mark them as correct when they touch your palm with their nose.

3. Reward by tossing a treat away from your dog when they touch your palm.

4. When they get the treat, encourage them to come back to you and have them Touch and toss another treat.

Paw

Verbal Cues
Paw and Shake

Visual Cue
Palm facing up,
slightly cupped,
moving toward paw

Teaching your dog to put their paw on your hand is a lovable classic trick. Many people know this cue so having it on hand is fun. Some dogs will learn paw more quickly than others. Some dogs "think" more with their paws than others, so if they have never been asked to touch something with their paw, it may take a bit of time to learn. If your dog has a certain toy or game that makes them offer more paw movement, use that item during training. Remember that a reward can be anything that your dog loves. Be sure to use a high-value treat when teaching this trick.

How Long Will It Take? 10 repetitions two times per day for four weeks for each visual and verbal cue

1. Hold a treat in your hand in a closed fist near one of your dog's shoulders.

2. They will try to get the treat out of your hand with their paw. When their paw touches your hand, mark them as correct with your clicker or marker word.

3. Reward with a treat.

Mark as correct when your dog moves their paw any amount.

Hold the treat slightly out of reach and see if one of your dog's front paws will come off the floor even just a tiny bit.

Mark them as correct for any subtle movement of their paw coming off the floor.

1. Pretend to have a treat in your fist and hold it out. Wait for your dog to paw at your fist.

2. Mark your dog as correct when they paw your hand.

3. Reward with a treat.

4. Open up your hand gradually over several repetitions until your dog is offering their paw to your open hand.

1. Next, teach your dog how to distinguish between their right and left paw with a visual cue. Hold your right hand near your dog's left paw. Your hand should be open with a flat palm facing downward, moving down.

2. If they offer their right paw, pull the treat away and try again.

3. When they offer their left paw, mark and reward.

4. Hold your left hand near your dog's right paw and give the visual cue again.

5. If they offer their left paw, pull the treat away and try again.

6. When they offer their right paw, mark and reward.

HOW TO ADD A VERBAL CUE

1. Say the verbal cue "Paw" one time just before using your right hand to show the visual cue to your dog. If they offer their right paw, pull the treat away and try again.

2. When they offer their left paw to your right hand, mark and reward with a treat.

3. Say the verbal cue "Shake" one time just before using your left hand to show the visual cue to your dog.

4. If they offer their left paw, pull the treat away and try again.

5. When they offer their right paw, mark and reward.

6. When your dog begins to respond to the verbal cue consistently, start to add a pause after you say the verbal cue to give your dog time to offer the correct behavior.

7. When your dog begins to respond consistently to the cues, you can pick either the verbal or visual cue to ask them for a Paw or a Shake.

Watch

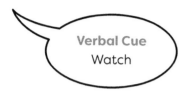

Verbal Cue
Watch

Visual Cue
Hand to collarbone

Teaching your dog to give you eye contact is necessary to keep their focus while training. Your dog must feel that paying attention to you is incredibly rewarding. Without your dog's attention, it is impossible to teach them anything. Attention is known as the mother of all behaviors. Be sure to practice this behavior often so your dog finds it very rewarding.

How Long Will It Take? 10 repetitions two times per day for four weeks for each visual and verbal cue

1. Start by showing your dog that you have a delicious treat. Lure your dog's gaze up toward your face by bringing your hand with the treat up toward your collarbone.

2. When your dog looks up at you, mark them as correct with your clicker or marker word.

3. Reward with a treat.

4. After your dog is offering eye contact, hold your hand with the treat about six inches or so from your face. Try to wait for your dog to look at you and then mark and reward. If you need to, you can make a kissy sound at first to lure their gaze.

NEED HELP?

Be sure that your dog understands that they must look at your eyes. Don't reward if they are looking at the treat.

At first, reward the moment your eyes meet before you begin to add duration.

HOW TO WORK THE TREAT OUT OF YOUR CUE HAND

1. Pinch a treat between your thumb and fingertips in both hands.

2. Place your left hand behind your back.

3. Bring your right hand toward your collarbone, then lure your dog to Watch.

4. Mark your dog as correct when they make eye contact.

5. Reward with a treat from your left hand.

6. Take the treats out of your right hand. Pretend to have a treat in your right hand and ask for Watch again.

7. Mark when they make eye contact and reward from your left hand.

8. Repeat with your left hand giving the cue and your right hand behind your back. Keep practicing until your dog responds consistently when you use an empty cue hand.

HOW TO ADD A VISUAL CUE

1. Pretend to have a treat in your hand and bring it up toward your collarbone.

2. When your dog offers eye contact, mark them as correct.

3. Reward with a treat from the opposite hand.

HOW TO ADD A VERBAL CUE

1. Say the verbal cue "Watch" one time just before showing the visual cue to your dog.

2. Mark when your dog makes eye contact.

3. Reward with a treat.

4. When your dog begins to respond to the verbal cue consistently, start to add a pause after you say the verbal cue to give your dog time to offer the correct behavior.

5. When your dog begins to respond consistently to the cues, you can pick either the verbal or visual cue to ask them to Watch.

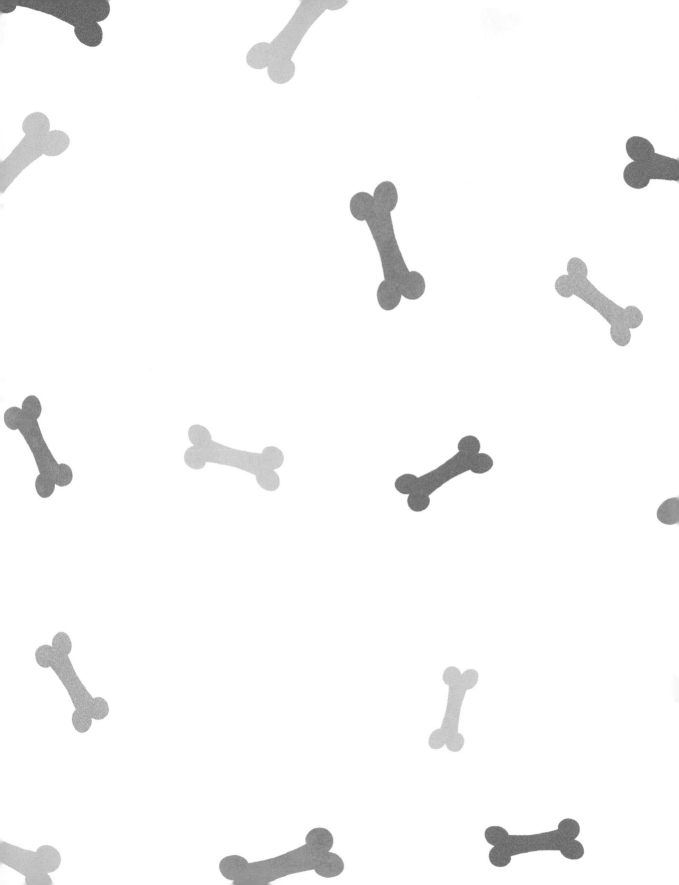

CHAPTER 3

Cool and Easy

Now that you have covered the basics, you and your dog are ready for the rest of the tricks in this guide! Here you will use the building blocks you learned in chapter 2 (see page 13) as the foundation of each new trick. Each trick indicates which foundational tricks are required to learn it as well as the difficulty level. As you begin to learn more intricate behaviors, remember to limit your sessions to 10 or 15 minutes and use a variety of high-value rewards. Shaping a behavior by marking each small movement in the direction of your end goal will help if you are having problems. These tricks will take multiple days, if not weeks, for your dog to learn. Remember that the learning times are estimates and can differ greatly from dog to dog. Be patient with your dog as they are trying to figure out what you are asking of them and have fun!

High-Five

Difficulty Level: Easy

Verbal Cue
High-Five

Visual Cue
Open, flat palm
giving a high-five

Required Tricks
Sit, Paw

High-Five is a cute move and makes a great party trick. Kids especially love this trick because it mimics a human behavior that they know. For a High-Five, you will get your dog to touch their paw to your hand when you hold it out as if giving a high-five to another person. Your dog will need to know Sit (see page 14) and Paw (see page 27) before being able to learn this trick.

How Long Will It Take? 10 repetitions two times per day for three weeks for each visual and verbal cue

1. Warm up your dog by practicing Paw.

2. Once your dog offers Paw consistently, prompt them to offer it again but present your hand a bit higher than you would for Paw. This encourages your dog to lift their paw up to touch your hand.

3. When your dog's paw touches your hand, mark them as correct with your clicker or marker word.

4. Reward with a treat.

NEED HELP?

Hold the treat in a fist near your dog's shoulder. Slowly open up your cue hand to a flat palm over several repetitions.

HOW TO ADD A VISUAL CUE

1. After warming up with Paw, hold your hand in a High-Five position near your dog's shoulder and wait for them to paw at it.

2. Mark your dog as correct when they give you a high-five.

3. Reward with a treat.

HOW TO ADD A VERBAL CUE

1. Say the verbal cue "High-Five" one time just before presenting a high-five to your dog.

2. Mark when your dog touches their paw to your hand.

3. Reward with a treat.

4. When your dog begins to respond to the verbal cue consistently, start to add a pause after you say "High-Five" to give your dog time to offer the correct behavior.

5. When your dog begins to respond consistently to the cues, you can pick either the verbal or visual cue to ask them for a High-Five.

Spin

Difficulty Level: Easy

Verbal Cues
Spin, Right, Left

Visual Cue
Pointing index finger
toward the ground
and moving in a
small circle

Required Tricks
Stand

A Spin cues your dog to walk in a circle on command. When you start to teach this trick, your dog will be following the treat to try to get it. Be sure to fade the lure quickly so that your dog doesn't become too dependent on seeing the treat. You can choose the cues "Left" and "Right," which makes it seem like your dog can understand directions! This trick is easy to learn and fun to practice.

How Long Will It Take? 10 repetitions two times per day for four weeks for each visual and verbal cue

1. Hold your hand up as if showing the number one.

2. Pinch a treat between your thumb and fingers.

3. Point your finger toward the ground and hold a treat next to your dog's nose.

4. Slowly arc the treat from their mouth toward their tail.

5. Continue to bring a treat around until they complete a full circle.

6. Mark your dog as correct with your clicker or marker word just as they complete a full circle.

7. Reward with a treat.

8. Repeat in the other direction.

NEED HELP?

Keep the treat at your dog's nose level to prevent them from jumping up or lying down.

Move slowly and reward for small steps in the correct direction.

HOW TO WORK THE TREAT OUT OF YOUR CUE HAND

1. Pinch a treat between your thumb and fingertips in both hands.

2. Place your left hand behind your back.

3. Lure your dog to Spin with your right hand.

4. Mark your dog as correct when they complete the circle.

5. Reward with a treat from your left hand.

6. Take the treats out of your right hand. Pretend to have a treat in your right hand and ask for Spin again.

7. Mark when they spin and reward from your left hand.

8. Repeat with your left hand giving the cue and your right hand behind your back.

HOW TO ADD A VISUAL CUE

1. Show your dog your hand pointing your index finger toward the ground and moving in a small circle, then lure them into the Spin using a treat to remind them of the behavior.

2. Mark when your dog completes the circle.

3. Reward with a treat.

4. When your dog begins to respond to the visual cue consistently, start to add a pause after you show your dog the visual cue to give them time to offer the correct behavior.

5. Mark your dog as correct when your dog Spins and reward with a treat.

6. Repeat in the other direction.

HOW TO ADD A VERBAL CUE

1. Say the verbal cue "Spin right" one time just before showing the visual cue to your dog.

2. Mark when your dog spins to the right.

3. Reward with a treat.

4. When your dog begins to respond to the verbal cue consistently, start to add a pause after you say the verbal cue to give your dog time to offer the correct behavior.

5. When your dog begins to respond consistently to the cues, you can pick either the verbal or visual cue to ask them for a Spin.

6. Repeat the steps for a left spin using the verbal cue "Spin left."

Difficulty Level: Easy

Verbal Cue
Stay

Visual Cue
Pointing index finger
as if showing the
number one

Required Tricks
Sit (with Duration),
Down

Being able to cue your dog to stay is a really valuable behavior. Not only is Stay a necessary cue to know for many tricks, it is also a helpful safety cue. Being able to quickly ask your dog to Stay could prevent them from running into harm. Working on Stay also helps your dog to build up impulse control and patience. You can create all kinds of games to play with your dog to work on Stay such as cueing the Stay and then trying to walk a circle around your dog without them getting up. This first trick is a Sit Stay, but you can also teach your dog to Down Stay.

How Long Will It Take? 10 repetitions two times per day for three weeks for each visual and verbal cue

TRY THIS (SIT STAY)

1. Cue your dog to Sit with a verbal or visual cue.

2. Start by moving one of your feet while your dog stays in a Sit.

3. Mark your dog as correct with your clicker or marker word if they stay.

4. Reward with a treat.

5. If your dog gets up, cue them back into a Sit and try again.

6. Once they are successful when you move one foot a bit, try taking one step back.

7. If your dog stays, mark and reward. If your dog gets up, cue them back into a Sit and try again.

8. As they get the hang of the exercise, take more steps back away from them.

9. When you are ready to release them, say, "Okay," and then mark and reward for getting up.

TRY THIS (DOWN STAY)

1. Cue your dog Down with a verbal or visual cue.

2. Start by trying to rock your weight back into one of your feet while your dog stays Down.

3. Mark your dog as correct with your clicker or marker word if they stay.

4. Reward with a treat.

5. If your dog gets up, cue them back to a Down and try again.

6. Once they are successful when you shift your weight, try taking one step back from your dog.

7. If your dog stays, mark and reward. If your dog gets up, cue them back into a Down and try again.

8. As they get the hang of the exercise, take more steps back away from them.

9. When you are ready to release them, say, "Okay," then mark and reward for getting up.

Try to barely move your feet at first. Mark and reward when your dog stays.

HOW TO ADD A VISUAL CUE

1. After cueing the Sit or Down, show your dog your index finger as if showing the number one.

2. Before you move, relax your arm by your side and then take one step back from your dog.

3. Mark when your dog stays.

4. Reward with a treat.

5. When your dog begins to respond to the visual cue consistently, start to add a pause after you show your dog the visual cue to give them time to offer the correct behavior.

6. Mark your dog as correct when your dog stays and reward with a treat.

7. If they get up or move without your "Okay," reset and try again.

HOW TO ADD A VERBAL CUE

1. After cueing the Sit or Down, say the verbal cue "Stay" one time just before showing the visual cue to your dog.

2. Mark when your dog stays.

3. Reward with a treat.

4. When your dog begins to respond to the verbal cue consistently, start to add a pause after you say the verbal cue to give your dog time to offer the correct behavior.

5. When your dog begins to respond consistently to the cues, you can pick either the verbal or visual cue to ask them for a Stay.

Roll Over

Difficulty Level: Intermediate

Verbal Cue
Roll Over

Visual Cue
Drawing a circle
in the air with your
index finger

Required Tricks
Down

This classic trick is always a crowd favorite. In a Roll Over, your dog lies on the ground, rolls onto their back, and flips over onto the other side. This trick is relatively easy to learn, but may take some practice if your dog isn't comfortable on their back. Work slowly and reward for each step in the right direction. Your dog may need to build up strength to offer this trick smoothly. Be sure to practice only a few repetitions each day until your dog has built up some core strength.

How Long Will It Take? 10 repetitions two times per day for four weeks for each visual and verbal cue

1. Ask for a Down with a verbal or visual cue.

2. Hold a treat close to your dog's nose, then slowly curve the treat toward one of your dog's shoulders. When your dog's nose moves toward their shoulder, their weight will shift onto one of their hips, creating a C curve with their body.

3. Let your dog nibble or lick at the treat and slowly bring it across your dog's shoulder line, which will cause them to roll onto their back with their belly up.

4. Keep bringing the treat slowly across the chest until your dog rolls all the way over to the other side.

5. Mark your dog as correct with your clicker or marker word when they are finishing up the roll.

6. Reward with a treat.

7. Repeat to the opposite shoulder and roll to the other side.

If your dog keeps getting up, try to shape the behavior by rewarding them while they are in a Down. Continue to reward for any movement of their head toward their shoulder.

Keep practicing shifting your dog's weight onto one hip and then slowly lure the roll.

1. Pinch a treat between your thumb and fingertips in both hands.

2. Place your left hand behind your back.

3. Cue a Down, then lure your dog to Roll Over with your right hand.

4. Mark your dog as correct when they roll all the way over to the other side.

5. Reward with a treat from your left hand.

6. Take the treats out of your right hand. Cue a Down. Pretend to have a treat in your right hand and ask for Roll Over again.

7. Mark when they Roll Over and reward from your left hand.

8. Repeat with your left hand giving the cue and your right hand behind your back.

HOW TO ADD A VISUAL CUE

1. Show your dog your hand drawing a circle in the air with your index finger, then lure them into the Roll Over using a treat to remind them of the behavior.

2. Mark when your dog rolls all the way over to the other side.

3. Reward with a treat.

4. When your dog begins to respond to the visual cue consistently, start to add a pause after you show your dog the visual cue to give them time to offer the correct behavior.

5. Mark your dog as correct when your dog Rolls Over and reward with a treat.

HOW TO ADD A VERBAL CUE

1. Say the verbal cue "Roll Over" one time just before showing the visual cue to your dog.

2. Mark when your dog Rolls Over.

3. Reward with a treat.

4. When your dog begins to respond to the verbal cue consistently, start to add a pause after you say the verbal cue to give your dog time to offer the correct behavior.

5. When your dog begins to respond consistently to the cues, you can pick either the verbal or visual cue to ask them for a Roll Over.

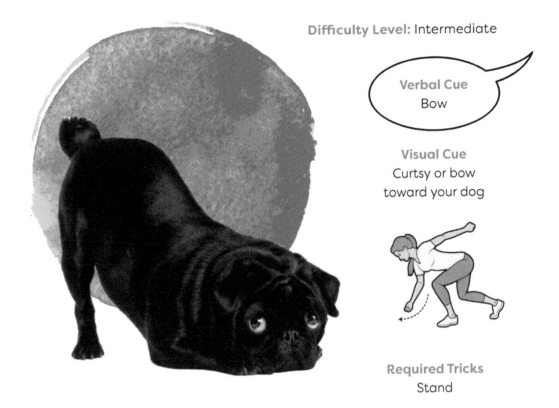

Difficulty Level: Intermediate

Verbal Cue
Bow

Visual Cue
Curtsy or bow
toward your dog

Required Tricks
Stand

In canine speak, a Bow is an invitation to play. This greeting is valuable for your dog to know. You can cue your dog to bow to send a friendly vibe to another dog. You may notice that your dog naturally offers this behavior when they wake up in the morning. Capture this behavior by marking your dog when you notice them bowing, then reward them. See if you notice your dog doing this behavior, try to mark and reward it.

How Long Will It Take? 10 repetitions two times per day for four weeks for each visual and verbal cue

1. Ask your dog to Stand in front of you using a verbal or visual cue.

2. Hold the treat close to your dog's nose.

3. Very slowly bring the treat down toward the floor aiming between your dog's front paws and slightly in toward their chest. This motion will cause their chest to drop and their rear to stay up in the air.

4. Mark your dog as correct with your clicker or marker word when their chest drops down while their hind end stays up.

5. Reward with a treat.

6. If their rear drops down, do not reward and try again.

Move slowly while you lure your dog into the Bow. If your dog moves too quickly, their rear will go down to the floor.

1. Cue your dog to Stand. Pinch a treat between your thumb and fingertips in both hands.

2. Place your left hand behind your back.

3. Lure your dog to Bow with your right hand.

4. Mark your dog as correct when their chest drops down while their hind end stays up.

5. Reward with a treat from your left hand.

6. Take the treats out of your right hand. Pretend to have a treat in your right hand and ask for the Bow again.

7. Mark when they Bow and reward from your left hand.

8. Repeat with your left hand giving the cue and your right hand behind your back.

1. Have your dog face you and curtsy or bow toward them, then lure them into the Bow using a treat to remind them of the behavior.

2. Mark when your dog Bows.

3. Reward with a treat.

4. When your dog begins to respond to the visual cue consistently, start to add a pause after you show your dog the visual cue to give them time to offer the correct behavior.

5. Mark your dog as correct when your dog Bows and reward with a treat.

1. Say the verbal cue "Bow" one time just before showing the visual cue to your dog.

2. Mark when your dog Bows.

3. Reward with a treat.

4. When your dog begins to respond to the verbal cue consistently, start to add a pause after you say the verbal cue to give your dog time to offer the correct behavior.

5. When your dog begins to respond consistently to the cues, you can pick either the verbal or visual cue to ask them for a Bow.

Sit Pretty

Difficulty Level: Advanced

Verbal Cue
Sit Pretty

Visual Cue
Fist moving up

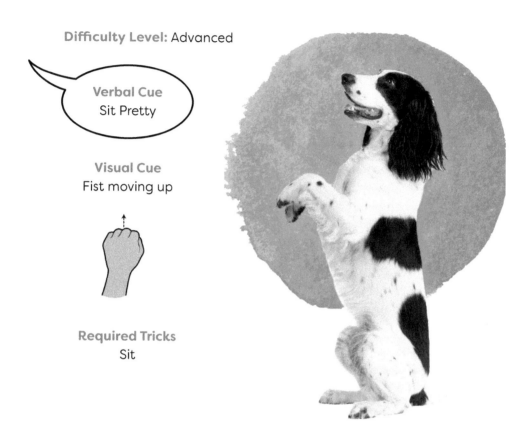

Required Tricks
Sit

In a Sit Pretty, your dog keeps their rear on the ground while lifting up their torso and paws so that they are sitting upright. This trick will take time to learn as it requires some core strength. It is especially important to only practice this trick 10 to 20 times per day for the first few weeks that you are working on it. This trick will help your dog have better balance and will help protect their spine from injury. Later on, you will use Sit Pretty for more advanced tricks like Monkey (see page 150) and Hug (see page 102). At first, reward for every small movement the dog's paws make off the ground. As your dog builds up their muscles, you will ask them to raise their chest and paws up. It is important to have your dog use good form with this trick so that they can build up the correct muscles.

How Long Will It Take? 10 repetitions two times per day for four weeks for each visual and verbal cue

1. Cue your dog into a Sit position. Make sure that their weight is distributed evenly on both hips. This is called "sitting square."

2. Hold a treat slightly above your dog's nose so that they extend their head and nose to try to reach the treat.

3. Slowly raise the treat about a half inch to an inch above their nose. As you do so, your dog will try to get the treat by lifting up their paws and torso.

4. Mark your dog as correct with your clicker or marker word the moment they lift a paw off the ground while keeping their rear down.

5. Reward with a treat.

6. As your dog becomes more comfortable and gains a bit of core strength, you can start to ask them to sit up higher and balance for longer.

NEED HELP?

Be sure to hold the treat an inch or two above the dog's head. Holding the treat too high can cause the dog to jump up. Reward at first the moment your dog lifts both paws off the ground.

HOW TO WORK THE TREAT OUT OF YOUR CUE HAND

1. Cue your dog into a Sit position. Pinch a treat between your thumb and fingertips in both hands.

2. Place your left hand behind your back.

3. Lure your dog to Sit Pretty with your right hand.

4. Mark your dog as correct when they lift their paws off the ground while keeping their rear down.

5. Reward with a treat from your left hand.

6. Take the treats out of your right hand. Pretend to have a treat in your right hand and ask for Sit Pretty again.

7. Mark when they offer a Sit Pretty and reward from your left hand.

8. Repeat with your left hand giving the cue and your right hand behind your back.

HOW TO ADD A VISUAL CUE

1. Show your dog a fist moving up, then lure them into Sit Pretty using a treat to remind them of the behavior.

2. Mark when your dog Sits Pretty.

3. Reward with a treat.

4. When your dog begins to respond to the visual cue consistently, start to add a pause after you show your dog the visual cue to give them time to offer the correct behavior.

5. Mark your dog as correct when your dog Sits Pretty and reward with a treat.

HOW TO ADD A VERBAL CUE

1. Say the verbal cue "Sit Pretty" one time just before showing the visual cue to your dog.

2. Mark when your dog Sits Pretty.

3. Reward with a treat.

4. When your dog begins to respond to the verbal cue consistently, start to add a pause after you say the verbal cue to give your dog time to offer the correct behavior.

5. When your dog begins to respond consistently to the cues, you can pick either the verbal or visual cue to ask them for a Sit Pretty.

Difficulty Level: Advanced

Verbal Cue
High-Ten

Visual Cue
Two flat open palms

Required Tricks
Sit, High-Five

For this trick, you will build on your work with High-Five (see page 36) to get your dog to touch both paws to your hands in a High-Ten.

How Long Will It Take? 20 repetitions two times per day for three weeks

TRY THIS

1. Cue your dog to Sit.

2. Cue a High-Five with your right hand and your dog's left paw.

3. Quickly bring your left hand near their right paw.

4. Mark your dog as correct with your clicker or marker word when they have both paws on your hands.

5. Reward with a treat.

NEED HELP?

Work on getting your dog to touch one of their paws to your hands before you ask them to touch both.

Once the dog has contact with one hand, they are balancing a bit and so making contact with their other paw is easy.

HOW TO ADD A VISUAL CUE

1. Show your dog two flat, open palms and ask them to High-Five each hand.

2. Mark when your dog has both paws on your hands.

3. Reward with a treat.

4. When your dog begins to respond to the visual cue consistently, start to add a pause after you show your dog the visual cue to give them time to offer the correct behavior.

5. Mark your dog as correct when your dog gives you a High-Ten and reward with a treat.

1. Say the verbal cue "High-Ten" one time just before showing the visual cue to your dog.

2. Mark when your dog touches their paws to your hands.

3. Reward with a treat.

4. When your dog begins to respond to the verbal cue consistently, start to add a pause after you say the verbal cue to give your dog time to offer the correct behavior.

5. When your dog begins to respond consistently to the cues, you can pick either the verbal or visual cue to ask them for a High-Ten.

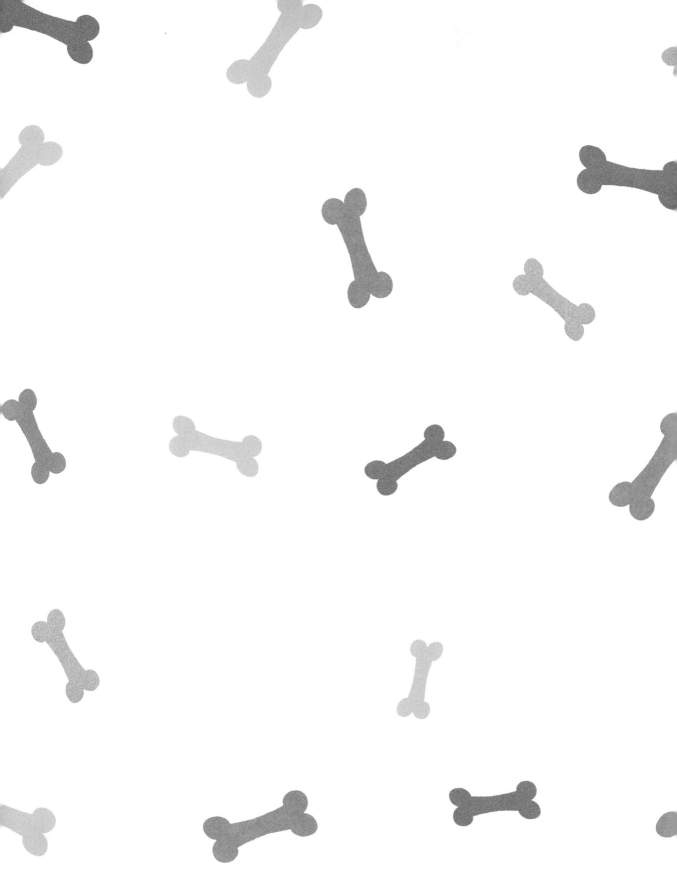

CHAPTER 4

Jump and Catch

In this chapter, you will learn tricks that will teach your dog how to get air off the ground and how to catch. You will also learn a few paw targeting exercises like Perch. When learning tricks with jumps, it is important that you only practice 5 to 10 repetitions per session to ensure that your dog keeps good form, preventing injury. Jumps are used in many tricks, such as Arm Hoop Jumps (see page 175) and Jump Over Legs (see page 76). Both jumping and catching are naturally satisfying to your dog, making these tricks enjoyable for them.

Get It

Difficulty Level: Easy

Verbal Cue
Get It

Visual Cue
Presenting an object
while saying the
verbal cue

Required Tricks
None

This exercise teaches your dog how to hold on to an object with their mouth. Learning this cue is the start of teaching your dog how to fetch. Get It is a really helpful cue to have in your back pocket for tricks such as Get Your Leash (see page 123) and Clean Up: Put Your Toys Away (see page 120). You can use Get It for making up your own retrieval tricks, and it is a great one to show off to your friends.

How Long Will It Take? 10 repetitions two times per day for four weeks for each visual and verbal cue

1. Hold a toy that your dog loves to play with and shake it or move it slowly in a snakelike pattern on the floor.

2. Mark your dog as correct with your clicker or marker word when they grab onto the toy with their mouth.

3. Reward with playing some tug with your dog.

4. As you practice, increase the amount of time that the dog is required to hold on to the toy before you mark them as correct.

NEED HELP?

If your dog is not interested in the toy, bring it to life by moving it around on the floor. This will tap into your dog's prey drive and will get them interested in putting their mouth on it. You can also use a treat to reward your dog when they grab onto the toy.

HOW TO ADD A VERBAL CUE

1. Say the verbal cue "Get It" one time just before you present the toy to your dog.

2. Mark when your dog grabs onto the toy with their mouth.

3. Reward with playing a bit of tug.

4. Slowly increase the amount of time that your dog must hold on to the toy before you mark them as correct.

Difficulty Level: Easy

Verbal Cue
Drop It

Visual Cue
None

Required Tricks
Get It

Teaching your dog to drop an item out of their mouth is an important behavior for their safety. If you have the ability to get your dog to let go of something, you can protect them from potentially swallowing something dangerous. Drop It is useful for learning tricks like Clean Up: Put Your Toys Away (see page 120).

How Long Will It Take? 10 repetitions two times per day for four weeks

1. Cue Get It or encourage your dog to grab onto a toy by moving it around.

2. Show your dog a treat or present a second toy to your dog to encourage them to open their jaw and release the toy.

3. Mark your dog as correct with your clicker or marker word the moment they release the toy.

4. Reward with a treat or toy.

You can also use a toy as the reward.

Try using two toys and exchange them instead of using a treat.

Let your arm go limp and stop playing tug when you want your dog to drop what they have in their mouth.

1. Cue your dog to Get It.

2. Pretend you have a treat and hold it near your dog's nose to encourage them to release their jaw.

3. Mark your dog as correct the moment they release the toy.

4. Reward with a treat or toy.

1. After your dog has a toy in their mouth, say the verbal cue "Drop It" one time just before showing your dog a treat.

2. Mark your dog as correct when they drop the toy.

3. Reward with a treat.

4. When your dog responds to the verbal cue consistently, add a pause after you say the verbal cue to give your dog time to offer correct behavior.

Fetch

Difficulty Level: Easy

Verbal Cue
Fetch

Visual Cue
None

Required Tricks
Get It, Drop It

Playing fetch is a fantastic way to give your dog exercise with some structure. Not only is fetch fun for your dog, but it is engaging and entertaining for you as well. Now that you have learned "Get It" and "Drop It" you can start to chain behaviors together to teach a solid retrieve behavior to your dog. To teach this trick, you will use back chaining, a technique in which you teach the final behavior first. This method is extremely effective in teaching complex behaviors and routines to your pup.

How Long Will It Take? 10 repetitions two times per day for three weeks

1. Toss a toy to your dog.

2. Cue Get It. When your dog gets the toy, praise them and encourage them to come back to you.

3. When they come back to you, give them a treat in exchange for the toy and toss it again.

4. If they do not give you the toy, cue Drop It.

Some dogs respond better when you use two toys instead of a treat. Have your dog get Toy 1 and then say "drop" just before squeaking and throwing Toy 2. When your dog grabs Toy 2, say "drop" and then squeak and throw Toy 1 again.

Try using a lotus ball or a toy with treats inside to add motivation to get the toy.

When your dog picks up the item with their mouth, mark and praise them a lot.

If they aren't coming back to you after getting the item, try running away from them.

Catch

Difficulty Level: Easy

Verbal Cue
Catch

Visual Cue
None

Required Tricks
Sit, Stand

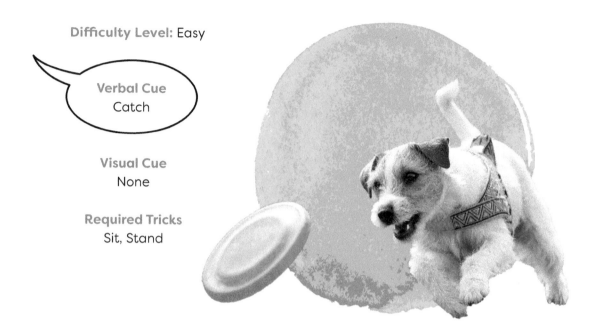

Believe it or not, you need to teach your dog how to Catch with their mouth. Catching requires your dog to use eye-and-mouth coordination, which takes practice. Stay patient with your dog and only ask them to Catch from short distances at first. It is important to keep them feeling successful. You can also try this exercise with a ball, disc, or toy.

How Long Will It Take? 10 repetitions two times per day for three weeks for each visual and verbal cue

1. Cue your dog to Sit or Stand. Hold a treat above your dog's head to encourage them to look up.

2. When your dog's mouth opens to eat the treat, drop the treat in their mouth.

3. Mark your dog as correct when they catch the treat in their mouth.

4. Raise a treat up slightly higher and try again.

5. Once your dog is offering to open their mouth for the treat, cue them into Sit or Stand and take a step or two back.

6. Toss the treat to them from a bit of a distance.

7. Mark your dog as correct with your clicker or marker word when they catch the treat.

8. Reward with a treat.

9. Once your dog catches treats consistently, start to use other objects such as a Frisbee or a ball.

NEED HELP?

Focus on marking the moment your dog opens their mouth before you drop the treat in.

Keep the treat one or two inches from your dog's mouth at first. Make it really easy for them before you start to make it harder.

HOW TO ADD A VERBAL CUE

1. Cue your dog to Sit or Stand. Say the verbal cue "Catch" one time just before tossing your dog a treat or toy.

2. Mark when your dog catches the object.

3. Reward with a treat.

4. When your dog begins to respond to the verbal cue consistently, start to add a pause after you say the verbal cue to give your dog time to offer the correct behavior.

5. When your dog begins to respond consistently to the cues, use the verbal cue to ask them to Catch.

Difficulty Level: Intermediate

Verbal Cue
Perch

Visual Cue
Pointing to an object with verbal cue "Perch"

Required Tricks
Stand

A "Perch" means that your dog puts their two front paws up on top of an object. You can be creative with what you use for perching, which keeps the trick interesting for you and your dog. I recommend using a pillow or hand towel to start with. Outdoors, you can ask your dog to perch on trees, walls, etc.

How Long Will It Take? 10 repetitions two times per day for two weeks for each visual and verbal cue

1. Have your dog stand near an object that they can put their paws on. Pick an object close to the ground at first, like a blanket, pillow, or towel. Fold it up into a rectangle near your dog.

2. Lure your dog with the treat to put their front two paws on the object.

3. Mark your dog as correct with your clicker or marker word when both of their paws are up on the object.

4. Reward your dog with a treat.

5. Once they offer the behavior consistently, lure them to Perch on higher objects such as stacked pillows, a bench, or a stair.

You can start to shape this behavior by marking and rewarding for one paw going near or on the object.

Use the treat to guide your dog slowly on to the object. Mark them when they touch either paw to the object. As they become more confident, start to encourage them to put both paws up before you reward them.

1. Pinch a treat between your thumb and fingertips in both hands.

2. Place your left hand behind your back.

3. Lure your dog to Perch on an object with your right hand pointing at the object.

4. Mark your dog as correct when both of their paws are on the object.

5. Reward with a treat from your left hand.

6. Take the treats out of your right hand. Pretend to have a treat in your left hand and ask for a Perch again by pointing to the object with your right hand.

7. Mark when they Perch and reward from your left hand.

8. Repeat with your left hand giving the cue and your right hand behind your back.

HOW TO ADD A VISUAL CUE

1. Show your dog the number one and point at an object, then lure them into the Perch on that object using a treat to remind them of the behavior.

2. Mark when your dog Perches.

3. Reward with a treat.

4. When your dog begins to respond to the visual cue consistently, start to add a pause after you show your dog the visual cue to give them time to offer the correct behavior.

5. Mark your dog as correct when your dog Perches and reward with a treat.

HOW TO ADD A VERBAL CUE

1. Say the cue word "Perch" one time just before pointing to the object you want your dog to perch on.

2. Mark when your dog Perches.

3. Reward with a treat.

4. When your dog begins to respond to the verbal cue consistently, start to add a pause after you say the verbal cue to give your dog time to offer the correct behavior.

5. When your dog begins to respond consistently to the cues, you can pick either the verbal or visual cue to ask them to Perch.

Contact: Back Legs On

Difficulty Level: Intermediate

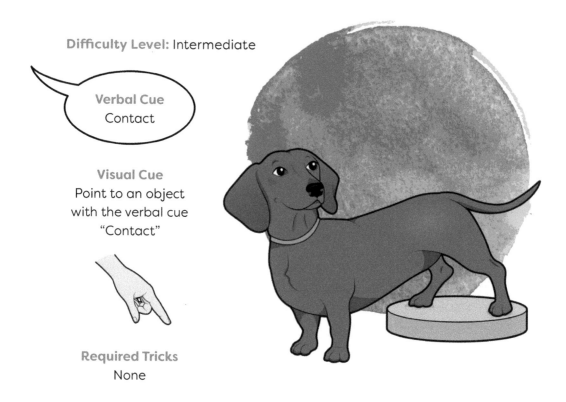

Verbal Cue
Contact

Visual Cue
Point to an object
with the verbal cue
"Contact"

Required Tricks
None

This behavior teaches your dog to put their back legs up on something. Many dogs have impressive front-end awareness, but have very little hind-end awareness. Working on having your dog put their hind legs up onto something is good preparation for agility obstacles. Once mastered, you can do amazing things with this behavior, such as teaching your dog to put their legs up on a wall.

How Long Will It Take? 10 repetitions two times per day for four weeks for each visual and verbal cue

1. Have your dog near an object that they can put their back legs on. Pick an object close to the ground at first like a blanket, pillow, or towel. Fold it up to create a small surface near your dog that they can fit both of their paws on.

2. Lure your dog to put their back two paws on the object by bringing your dog in front of the object and encouraging them to get on it with a treat so that their front paws touch, then continue to lure them until their back paws make contact.

3. Mark your dog as correct with your clicker or marker word when both back paws touch the object.

4. Reward your dog with a treat.

5. Once they offer the behavior consistently, lure them to Contact on higher objects such as a bench.

NEED HELP?

Get your dog to stand in the middle of the object before you lure them.

HOW TO WORK THE TREAT OUT OF YOUR CUE HAND

1. Pinch a treat between your thumb and fingertips in both hands.

2. Place your left hand behind your back.

3. Lure your dog to Contact an object with your right hand.

4. Mark your dog as correct when both of their back paws are on the object.

5. Reward with a treat from your left hand.

6. Take the treats out of your right hand. Pretend to have a treat in your right hand and ask for Contact again.

7. Mark when they Contact and reward from your left hand.

8. Repeat with your left hand giving the cue and your right hand behind your back.

HOW TO ADD A VISUAL CUE

1. Show your dog the number one and point to an object, then lure them into Contact on that object using a treat to remind them of the behavior.

2. Mark when your dog makes Contact with their back two paws.

3. Reward with a treat.

4. When your dog begins to respond to the visual cue consistently, start to add a pause after you show your dog the visual cue to give them time to offer the correct behavior.

5. Mark your dog as correct when your dog has their back two feet up and reward with a treat.

HOW TO ADD A VERBAL CUE

1. Say the cue word "Contact" one time just before pointing to the object you want your dog to Contact on.

2. Mark when your dog puts their back two paws up.

3. Reward with a treat.

4. When your dog begins to respond to the verbal cue consistently, start to add a pause after you say the verbal cue to give your dog time to offer the correct behavior.

5. When your dog begins to respond consistently to the cues, you can pick either the verbal or visual cue to ask them for a Contact.

Up: All Four Paws On

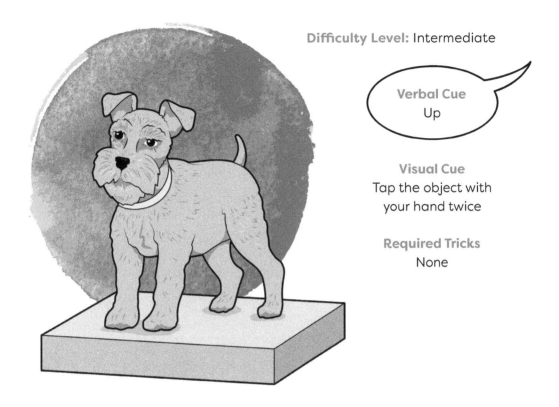

Difficulty Level: Intermediate

Verbal Cue
Up

Visual Cue
Tap the object with
your hand twice

Required Tricks
None

This trick teaches your dog to get up onto an object with all four paws. Working on paw awareness helps your dog navigate through life with ease and confidence. Be sure to only practice 5 to 10 repetitions of this behavior at a time if the object you are using requires the dog to jump.

How Long Will It Take? 10 repetitions two times per day for three weeks for each verbal and visual cue

TRY THIS

1. Have your dog near an object that they can put all four paws on. Pick an object close to the ground at first, like a blanket, pillow, or towel. Fold it up into a rectangle near your dog.

2. Lure your dog with the treat to encourage them to put their front paws on and then continue to lure until they have their back two paws on the object as well.

3. Mark your dog as correct with your clicker or marker word when all four paws are on.

4. Reward with a treat.

5. Once they offer the behavior consistently, lure them to get up on higher objects, such as a bench.

NEED HELP?

If your dog is hesitant, start by rewarding your dog for putting one paw on the object. Then try for two, then three, and then all four.

Set your dog up for success by making sure they are facing straight ahead in the center of the object.

If your dog seems nervous about the object, get a higher value treat and set a few pieces on the object. Let your dog inspect the object and eat treats off of it before you ask them to go back up.

HOW TO WORK THE TREAT OUT OF YOUR CUE HAND

1. Pinch a treat between your thumb and fingertips in both hands.

2. Place your left hand behind your back.

3. Lure your dog onto the object with your right hand.

4. Mark your dog as correct when all four paws are on the blanket.

5. Reward with a treat from your left hand.

6. Take the treats out of your right hand. Pretend to have a treat in your right hand and ask for your dog to get up.

7. Mark when they get up on the object with all fours and reward from your left hand.

8. Repeat with your left hand giving the cue and your right hand behind your back. Keep practicing until your dog responds consistently when you use an empty cue hand.

HOW TO ADD A VISUAL CUE

1. Tap the object with your hand twice, then lure your dog on to the object using a treat to remind them of the behavior.

2. Mark when your dog puts all four paws on the object.

3. Reward with a treat.

4. When your dog begins to respond to the visual cue consistently, start to add a pause after you show your dog the visual cue to give them time to offer the correct behavior.

5. Mark your dog as correct when your dog puts all four paws on and reward with a treat.

HOW TO ADD A VERBAL CUE

1. Say the verbal cue "Up" one time just before tapping the object twice with your hand.

2. Mark when your dog puts all four paws on the object.

3. Reward with a treat.

4. When your dog begins to respond to the verbal cue consistently, start to add a pause after you say the verbal cue to give your dog time to offer the correct behavior.

5. When your dog begins to respond consistently to the cues, you can pick either the verbal or visual cue to ask them to get up on objects with all four paws.

Jump Over Legs

Difficulty Level: Easy

Verbal Cue
Jump

Visual Cue
A finger pointing
over your legs

Required Tricks
None

Asking your dog to jump over your legs is a cool trick you can perform anywhere. This trick teaches your dog to jump over one or both of your legs on cue. The aerobic exercise is hard work physically for your dog and will tire them easily. Your dog should always be jumping in proper form—keeping their head and neck looking down—which keeps their spine in good alignment. Try this trick seated with your legs out flat on the ground at first. Once you begin to lift your leg, keep it only a foot or two off the ground. You can use a wall for back support if needed.

How Long Will It Take? 10 repetitions two times per day for four weeks for each visual and verbal cue

1. Sit on the floor and call your dog to come to you.

2. Reward them for coming, then lure them so that they are on one side of you, facing across your legs.

3. Raise your legs slightly off the ground, toss a treat over them to encourage your dog to jump over. (Tossing the treat encourages your dog to jump in the proper form by getting their head looking down.)

4. Mark your dog as correct when they jump over your leg.

5. Reward with a treat.

6. When your dog is consistently jumping over your legs while seated, stand up and lift one of your legs slightly off the ground.

7. Toss a treat over one of your legs to prompt your dog to jump over.

8. Mark your dog as correct when they jump over your leg.

9. Reward with a treat.

NEED HELP?

Try crossing one leg on top of the other to add a bit more height.

Keep your legs close to the ground while your dog is learning and building the correct muscles.

If your dog is having trouble transitioning to the standing jump, try sitting in a chair so your legs are lower. Then try standing again.

HOW TO ADD A VISUAL CUE

1. Hold a treat in your right hand behind your back.

2. Pretend like you have a treat in your left hand and move your hand across your legs.

3. Mark your dog as correct when they jump over your legs.

4. Repeat with a treat in your right hand and your left hand behind your back.

HOW TO ADD A VERBAL CUE

1. Say the verbal cue "Jump" one time just before showing the visual cue to your dog.

2. Mark when your dog jumps over your legs.

3. Reward with a treat.

4. When your dog begins to respond to the verbal cue consistently, start to add a pause after you say the verbal cue to give your dog time to offer the correct behavior.

5. When your dog begins to respond consistently to the cues, you can pick either the verbal or visual cue to ask them to jump over your legs.

Jump Over Arms

Difficulty Level: Easy

Verbal Cue
Jump

Visual Cue
Kneeling with an
arm out to the side

Required Tricks
Sit

This trick teaches your dog to jump over your arms. You can build on it to teach tricks later on, such as the Arm Hoop Jumps (see page 175). Try working with your arm touching a wall if needed. Never ask your dog to jump higher than two feet or so with this exercise.

How Long Will It Take? 10 repetitions two times per day for three weeks for each visual and verbal cue

1. Kneel on the floor and call your dog to you.

2. Cue your dog to Sit using a visual or verbal cue.

3. Keep your right elbow next to your side and hold your forearm parallel to the floor with your palm facing up.

4. Look over your right shoulder.

5. Hold a treat in your left hand and toss it over your right arm.

6. Mark your dog as correct with your clicker or marker word when they jump over your arm.

7. Reward with a treat.

Be sure to toss the treat to encourage good form while jumping.

Keep your arm low to the ground while your dog is learning the trick and developing the correct muscles.

1. Kneel on the floor and call your dog to you.

2. Cue your dog to Sit using a visual or verbal cue.

3. Keep your right elbow next to your side and hold your forearm parallel to the floor with your palm facing up.

4. Look over your right shoulder.

5. Pretend to hold a treat in your left hand and toss the pretend treat over your right arm.

6. Mark your dog as correct when they jump over your arm.

7. Reward with a treat.

8. Keep practicing until your dog responds consistently when you use an empty cue hand.

1. Say the verbal cue "Jump" one time just before presenting your arm to your dog.

2. Mark when your dog jumps over your arm.

3. Reward with a treat.

4. When your dog begins to respond to the verbal cue consistently, start to add a pause after you say the verbal cue to give your dog time to offer the correct behavior.

5. When your dog begins to respond consistently to the cues, you can pick either the verbal or visual cue to ask them to jump over your arms.

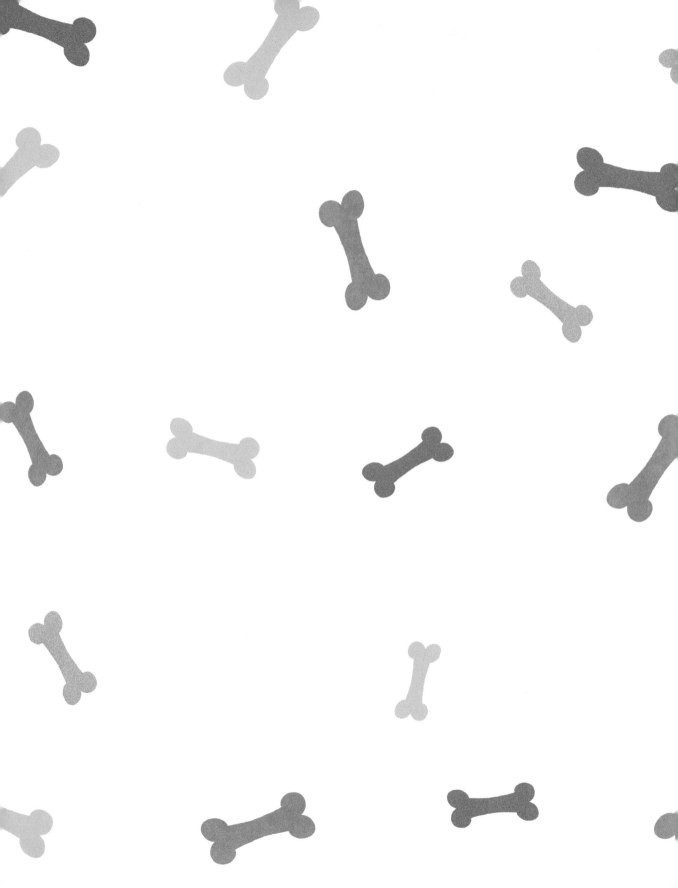

CHAPTER 5

Play It Cute

Do you dream of having a dog more famous than Lassie? Learn this chapter's tricks, get your camera ready, and you will be on your way. This chapter will teach you and your dog tricks that are unbelievably adorable. These crowd-pleasers are a joy to work on and will never fail to bring a smile to your face.

Snoot

Difficulty Level: Easy

Verbal Cue
Snoot

Visual Cue
Index finger and thumb touching with other fingers spread out, like an okay sign

Required Tricks
None

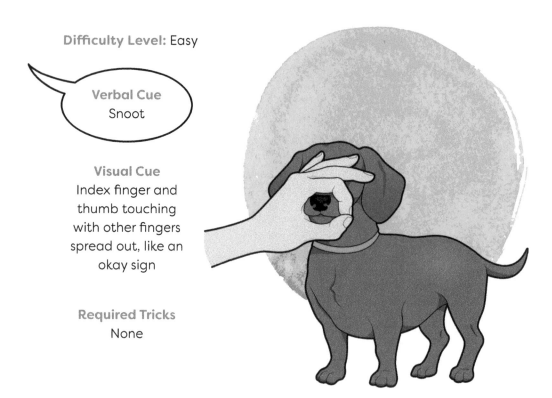

This trick became famous on social media in 2018 and is a party favorite! In this trick, you present your hand as if showing an okay sign to your dog and they will put their nose in the ring that your fingers are making. This trick is an easy one to teach a kid to perform and is so cute to watch.

How Long Will It Take? 10 repetitions two times per day for four weeks for each visual and verbal cue

1. Hold out your right hand with your index finger and thumb touching while holding your other fingers spread out, like an okay sign.

2. Hold a treat in your left hand just outside of your right hand.

3. Present both hands to your dog and encourage their nose to go through the hole made by your fingers.

4. Mark your dog as correct with your clicker or marker word when their nose goes through the hole.

5. Reward with a treat.

6. Switch hands and repeat.

NEED HELP?

Hold the treat and your visual cue an inch or two away from your dog at first before adding any distance to this trick.

HOW TO WORK THE TREAT OUT OF YOUR CUE HAND

1. Pinch a treat between your thumb and fingertips in both hands.

2. Place your left hand behind your back.

3. Lure your dog to put their nose through your fingers with your right hand.

4. Mark your dog as correct when their nose goes through the hole.

5. Reward with a treat from your left hand.

6. Take the treats out of your right hand. Pretend to have a treat in your right hand and ask for a Snoot again.

7. Mark when they Snoot and reward from your left hand. Repeat with your left hand giving the cue and your right hand behind your back. Keep practicing until your dog responds consistently when you use an empty cue hand.

HOW TO ADD A VERBAL CUE

1. Say the verbal cue "Snoot" one time just before showing the visual cue to your dog.

2. Mark when your dog puts their nose through your fingers.

3. Reward with a treat.

4. When your dog begins to respond to the verbal cue consistently, start to add a pause after you say the verbal cue to give your dog time to offer the correct behavior.

5. When your dog begins to respond consistently to the cues, you can pick either the verbal or visual cue to ask them for a Snoot.

Difficulty Level: Easy

Verbal Cue
Post

Visual Cue
Standing with legs slightly apart, one finger pointed down

Required Tricks
None

The Post trick is sometimes referred to as "Peek-a-Boo." It cues your dog to poke their head between your legs, which is always a crowd favorite. This trick can be used in routines or as a space saver in small spaces, such as in an elevator.

How Long Will It Take? 10 repetitions two times per day for four weeks for each visual and verbal cue

1. Stand with your legs slightly apart.

2. Hold a treat pinched in your fingers near your dog's nose.

3. Use the treat to lure your dog's head behind you and under your legs.

4. Mark your dog as correct with your clicker or marker word right when their head pokes through your legs. Let your dog walk all the way through or lure him through.

5. Reward with a treat.

NEED HELP?

Reward your dog the moment their head goes under your legs before they walk all the way through.

HOW TO WORK THE TREAT OUT OF YOUR CUE HAND

1. Hold a treat in both fists.

2. Place your left hand behind your back.

3. Stand up straight with your legs slightly apart and, with your right hand, point one finger down toward the ground in front of you. Look down in front of you to help show your dog where to go.

4. When your dog goes under your legs, mark them as correct.

5. Reward with a treat from your left hand.

6. Take the treats out of your right hand. Pretend to have a treat in your right hand and ask for Post again.

7. Mark when they go through your legs and reward from your left hand.

8. Repeat with your left hand giving the cue and your right hand behind your back. Keep practicing until your dog responds consistently when you use an empty cue hand.

1. Say the verbal cue "Post" one time just before getting into position with your legs slightly apart and one finger pointing down.

2. Mark when your dog pokes their head under your legs.

3. Reward with a treat.

4. When your dog begins to respond to the verbal cue consistently, start to add a pause after you say the verbal cue to give your dog time to offer the correct behavior.

5. When your dog begins to respond consistently to the cues, you can pick either the verbal or visual cue to ask them to Post.

Crawl

Difficulty Level: Easy

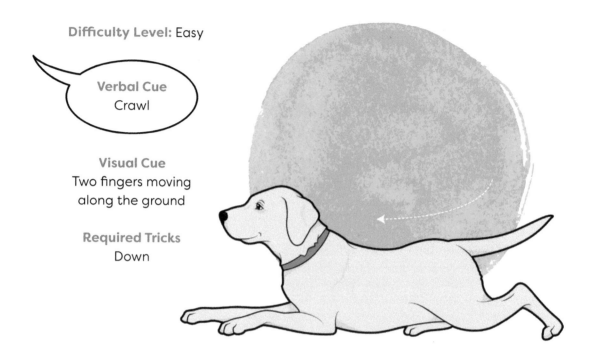

Verbal Cue
Crawl

Visual Cue
Two fingers moving
along the ground

Required Tricks
Down

Crawling is an athletic behavior that is hilarious to watch. This trick teaches your dog to move across the floor while keeping their belly on the ground. You will adore watching your dog learn this trick. A crawl is physically demanding so be sure to only practice 5 to 10 repetitions of this each session.

How Long Will It Take? 10 repetitions two times per day for four weeks for each visual and verbal cue

1. Cue your dog into a Down position.

2. With a treat pinched between your thumb and fingertips, bring your hand to the floor just in front of your dog and begin to slowly drag the treat along the floor away from your dog.

3. As your dog tries to get the treat, they will slide their body across the floor.

4. Mark your dog as correct with your clicker or marker word for any movement forward while keeping their belly on the floor.

5. As you progress, require your dog to move a bit farther forward before marking them as correct and rewarding.

NEED HELP?

If your dog's rear comes off the floor, take the treat away and try again.

If your dog is getting up, move the treat even more slowly.

Let your dog nibble or lick the treat as you move it.

HOW TO WORK THE TREAT OUT OF YOUR CUE HAND

1. Pinch a treat between your thumb and fingertips in both hands.

2. Place your left hand behind your back.

3. Lure your dog to Crawl with your right hand.

4. Mark your dog as correct when they move forward while keeping their belly on the floor.

5. Reward with a treat from your left hand.

6. Take the treats out of your right hand. Pretend to have a treat in your right hand and ask for a Crawl again.

7. Mark when they Crawl and reward from your left hand.

8. Repeat with your left hand giving the cue and your right hand behind your back. Keep practicing until your dog responds consistently when you use an empty cue hand.

HOW TO ADD A VISUAL CUE

1. Show your dog two fingers moving along the ground, then lure them into the Crawl using a treat to remind them of the behavior.

2. Mark when your dog Crawls.

3. Reward with a treat.

4. When your dog begins to respond to the visual cue consistently, start to add a pause after you show your dog the visual cue to give them time to offer the correct behavior.

5. Mark your dog as correct when your dog Crawls and reward with a treat.

HOW TO ADD A VERBAL CUE

1. Say the verbal cue "Crawl" one time just before showing the visual cue to your dog.

2. Mark when your dog Crawls.

3. Reward with a treat.

4. When your dog begins to respond to the verbal cue consistently, start to add a pause after you say the verbal cue to give your dog time to offer the correct behavior.

5. When your dog begins to respond consistently to the cues, you can pick either the verbal or visual cue to ask them for a Crawl.

Rest: Chin on Lap

Difficulty Level: Intermediate

Verbal Cue
Rest

Visual Cue
One hand on your lap

Required Tricks
Stand, Stay

This endearing trick cues your dog to rest their chin on your lap. This trick can be used during flights to keep your dog calm. If you plan on having your dog around children, elderly or frail people, this trick will encourage them to calmly greet people.

How Long Will It Take? 10 repetitions two times per day for four weeks for each visual and verbal cue

TRY THIS

1. If you have a small dog, you will need to be sitting on the ground or on a couch with them for this trick. If you have a medium or large dog, you will need to be sitting in a chair.

2. Cue your dog to Stand and Stay near your side with their head facing across your lap.

3. Use the treat to lure your dog's head over your lap and slightly down so that their chin rests on your lap.

4. Mark your dog as correct with your clicker or marker word when their head rests on your lap.

5. Reward with a treat.

NEED HELP?

Try placing a treat between your knees so that your dog makes contact between their head and your lap.

HOW TO WORK THE TREAT OUT OF YOUR CUE HAND

1. Pinch a treat between your thumb and fingertips in both hands.

2. Place your left hand behind your back.

3. Lure your dog to rest their chin on your lap. with your right hand.

4. Mark your dog as correct when they put their chin on your lap.

5. Reward with a treat from your left hand.

6. Take the treats out of your right hand. Pretend to have a treat in your right hand and ask for the Rest again.

7. Mark when they put their chin on your lap and reward from your left hand.

8. Repeat with your left hand giving the cue and your right hand behind your back. Keep practicing until your dog responds consistently when you use an empty cue hand.

HOW TO ADD A VISUAL CUE

1. Show your dog one hand on your lap, then lure them to rest their head on your lap using a treat to remind them of the behavior.

2. Mark when your dog places his chin on your lap.

3. Reward with a treat.

4. When your dog begins to respond to the visual cue consistently, start to add a pause after you show your dog the visual cue to give them time to offer the correct behavior.

5. Mark your dog as correct when your dog Rests and reward with a treat.

HOW TO ADD A VERBAL CUE

1. Say the verbal cue "Rest" one time just before showing the visual cue to your dog.

2. Mark when your dog rests their chin on your lap.

3. Reward with a treat.

4. When your dog begins to respond to the verbal cue consistently, start to add a pause after you say the verbal cue to give your dog time to offer the correct behavior.

5. When your dog begins to respond consistently to the cues, you can pick either the verbal or visual cue to ask them to Rest.

Wave

Difficulty Level: Advanced

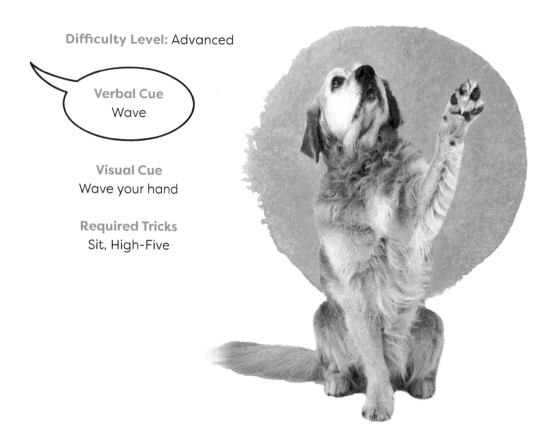

Verbal Cue
Wave

Visual Cue
Wave your hand

Required Tricks
Sit, High-Five

Have your dog wave hello and goodbye to you and your friends! Use this trick with your houseguests to make them feel welcomed. This trick is used often in movies and TV shows. Waving is a trick that will capture your heart.

How Long Will It Take? 10 repetitions two times per day for six weeks for each visual and verbal cue

1. Use a verbal or visual cue to prompt your dog to Sit.

2. Cue your dog to offer a High-Five.

3. Pull your hand away about one inch and quickly cue another High-Five.

4. Mark them as correct with your clicker or marker word when your dog offers a paw swat that looks like a wave.

5. Reward with a treat.

NEED HELP?

At first your dog will likely swat at your hand as you pull it away. Mark and reward the swatting action. As they get to know the trick, you will ask for two "swats" before marking and rewarding to create a wave pattern.

Pull your hand away even faster from your pup after they offer their paw.

HOW TO ADD A VISUAL CUE

1. Use a verbal or visual cue to prompt your dog to Sit.

2. Hold your hand up and make a wave motion with your fingers by opening and closing your hand.

3. If needed, show your dog a High-Five hand cue to encourage them to hold their paw up.

4. Mark them as correct when your dog offers two paw swats that look like a wave.

5. Reward with a treat.

HOW TO ADD A VERBAL CUE

1. Say the verbal cue "Wave" one time just before showing the visual cue to your dog.

2. Mark when your dog Waves.

3. Reward with a treat.

4. When your dog begins to respond to the verbal cue consistently, start to add a pause after you say the verbal cue to give your dog time to offer the correct behavior.

5. When your dog begins to respond consistently to the cues, you can pick either the verbal or visual cue to ask them for a Wave.

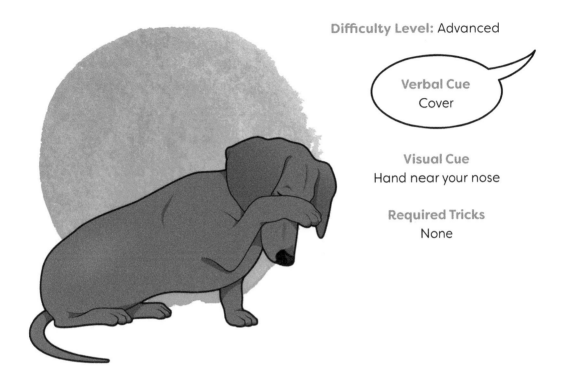

Difficulty Level: Advanced

Verbal Cue
Cover

Visual Cue
Hand near your nose

Required Tricks
None

This trick is guaranteed to give you a chuckle. You can use a simple verbal cue like "Cover" or you can get clever and use a cue such as "Who ate the cookies?" or "Don't look" to get your dog to cover their eyes. This may take weeks to get on cue, but it is well worth the work.

How Long Will It Take? 10 repetitions two times per day for five weeks for each visual and verbal cue

TRY THIS (METHOD 1)

1. Gently blow a tiny puff of air on the top of your dog's nose, which causes them to feel a little tickle on their nose.

2. Your dog will likely put their paw on their nose to scratch themselves.

3. When the paw makes contact with their nose, mark your dog as correct with your clicker or marker word.

4. Reward with a treat.

5. Pause and wait for your dog to offer their paw to their nose again without prompting them with air or tape.

6. Mark them as correct with your clicker or marker word when their paw touches their nose.

TRY THIS (METHOD 2)

1. Use a very tiny piece of basic scotch tape and roll it into a circle.

2. Very lightly set the tape on your dog's nose. To get it off, they will paw at their nose, covering their eyes. Mark when their paw touches their nose and reward with a treat.

3. Repeat five times, then try to wait until your dog offers their paw without tape.

4. When your dog puts their paw on their nose, mark them as correct with your clicker or marker word.

5. Reward with a treat.

NEED HELP?

You can also try using a sticky note.

If your dog shakes their head to get it off, try this in a Down position.

HOW TO ADD A VISUAL CUE

1. Warm your dog up with the puff of air or the tape for a few repetitions.

2. Put your hand near your nose and pause and see if they offer behavior on their own.

3. If they don't offer, prompt them again to offer paw to nose.

4. Mark your dog as correct when their paw touches their nose.

HOW TO ADD A VERBAL CUE

1. Say the verbal cue "Cover" one time just before showing the visual cue to your dog.

2. Mark when your dog puts their paw on their nose.

3. Reward with a treat.

4. When your dog begins to respond to the verbal cue consistently, start to add a pause after you say the verbal cue to give your dog time to offer the correct behavior.

5. When your dog begins to respond consistently to the cues, you can pick either the verbal or visual cue to ask them to Cover Your Eyes.

Hug

Difficulty Level: Advanced

Verbal Cue
Hug

Visual Cue
Kneeling with hands
reaching toward
your dog

Required Tricks
Sit, Sit Pretty,
High-Ten

What could be cuter than cueing your dog to give a big hug? After working on this trick, your dog will be able to give a hug to anyone. Once you have mastered Sit Pretty (see page 50), this trick should come fairly naturally to your dog. Practice daily until you reach your final goal. This trick will look amazing in photos!

How Long Will It Take? 10 repetitions two times per day for six weeks for each visual and verbal cue

1. While in a kneeling or sitting position, cue your dog to Sit in front of you.

2. Cue your dog to Sit Pretty.

3. Start by asking your dog for a High-Ten when they are in a Sit Pretty.

4. Mark your dog as correct with your clicker or marker word when they touch their paws to your hands.

5. Reward with a treat.

6. While your dog is in a Sit Pretty ask for a High-Ten and then start to reach your arms out toward their shoulder.

7. Mark your dog as correct with your clicker or marker word when your hand touches their shoulder and their paws touch your shoulder.

8. Reward with a delicious treat.

NEED HELP?

Reward your dog at first for any contact their paws make on your arms. As they get more confident with the behavior, you can shape the way you want their arms to look.

HOW TO ADD A VERBAL CUE

1. Say the verbal cue "Hug" one time just before kneeling and stretching your hands toward your dog.

2. Mark when your dog Hugs you.

3. Reward with a treat.

4. When your dog begins to respond to the verbal cue consistently, start to add a pause after you say the verbal cue to give your dog time to offer the correct behavior.

5. When your dog begins to respond consistently to the cues, you can pick either the verbal or visual cue to ask them for a Hug.

Up Tall

Difficulty Level: Intermediate

Verbal Cue
Up Tall

Visual Cue
Hand showing two
fingers, like the
"number-two" sign

Required Tricks
Sit Pretty

Teach your dog to stand up like a person with this trick. This is a physically challenging trick and may take a bit of core conditioning. After you teach your dog to stand on their hind legs, you can work on fun tricks like walking upright, dancing on hind legs, and other advanced behaviors.

How Long Will It Take? 10 repetitions two times per day for three weeks for both visual and verbal cues

1. Cue your dog to Sit Pretty with a lure.

2. Lift the treat up three or four inches above your dog's nose so that they must extend their back legs up.

3. Mark your dog as correct with a clicker or marker word when your dog is standing up.

NEED HELP?

Move the treat slowly up to guide your dog to lift up onto their hind legs.

HOW TO WORK THE TREAT OUT OF YOUR CUE HAND

1. Pinch a treat between your thumb and fingertips in both hands.

2. Place your left hand behind your back.

3. Cue your dog to Sit Pretty. Lure your dog to stand on their hind legs with your right hand.

4. Mark your dog as correct when they stand on their hind legs.

5. Reward with a treat from your left hand.

6. Take the treats out of your right hand. Pretend to have a treat in your left hand and ask for Up Tall again.

7. Mark when they stand on their hind legs and reward from your left hand.

8. Repeat with your left hand giving the cue and your right hand behind your back. Keep practicing until your dog responds consistently when you use an empty cue hand.

HOW TO ADD A VISUAL CUE

1. Cue your dog to Sit Pretty. Show your dog the number-two sign with a treat in your fist, then lure them into the Up Tall using the treat to remind them of the behavior.

2. Mark when your dog stands on their hind legs.

3. Reward with a treat.

4. When your dog begins to respond to the visual cue consistently, start to add a pause after you show your dog the visual cue to give them time to offer the correct behavior.

5. Mark your dog as correct when your dog stands on their hind legs and reward with a treat.

HOW TO ADD A VERBAL CUE

1. Say the verbal cue "Up Tall" one time just before showing the visual cue to your dog.

2. Mark when your dog stands on their hind legs.

3. Reward with a treat.

4. When your dog begins to respond to the verbal cue consistently, start to add a pause after you say the verbal cue to give your dog time to offer the correct behavior.

5. When your dog begins to respond consistently to the cues, you can pick either the verbal or visual cue to ask them for an Up Tall.

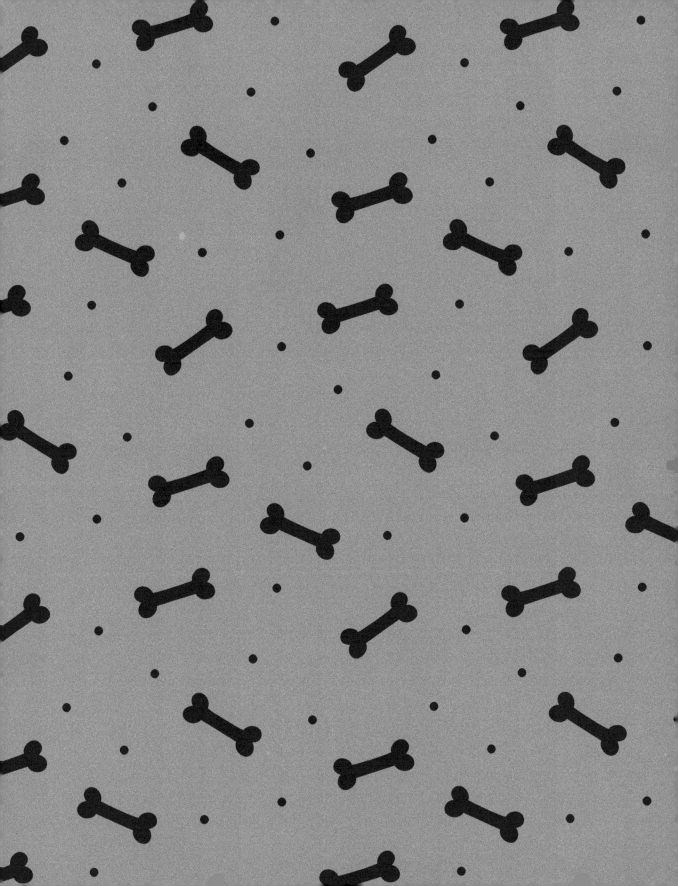

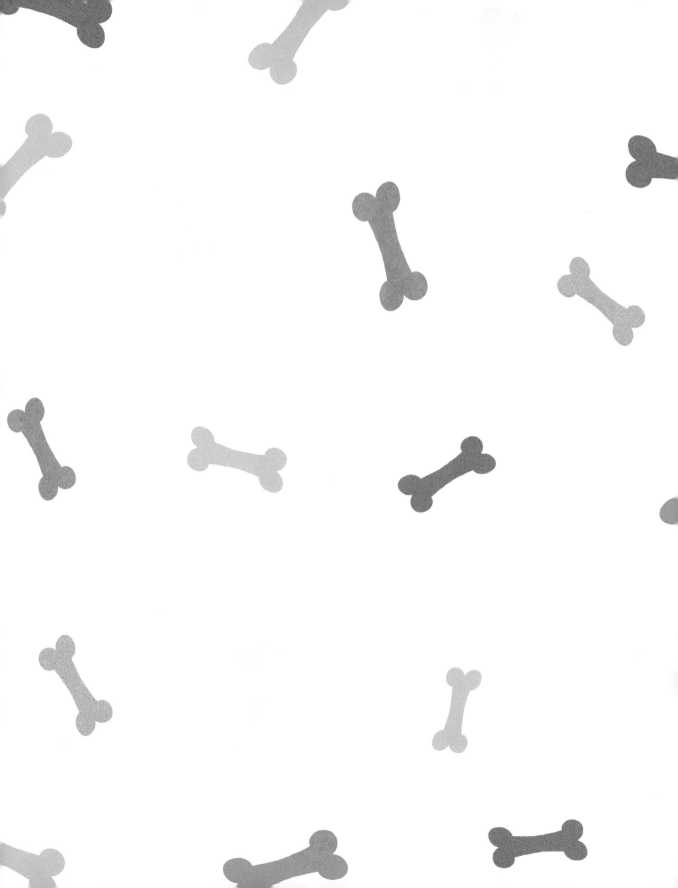

CHAPTER 6

Play It Smart

Exercise your dog's mind in new ways with this group of tricks that focuses on challenging your pup to do some serious brain work. In this chapter, your dog will learn tricks that focus on retrieving, searching, and speaking. Several of these tricks require your dog to have a solid "Get It" (see page 58) cue so be sure to brush up on that skill if needed. Some of the tricks in this chapter may take several months to learn, so it is important that you work on each trick daily to see improvement as quickly as possible. Make the training game fun for your dog and keep them feeling confident.

Speak

Difficulty Level: Easy

Verbal Cue
Speak

Visual Cue
Thumb touching
fingertips like a
duckbill, opening
and closing

Required Tricks
Sit

Barking on command is a practical trick to teach as it gives your dog an outlet for making noise. Being allowed to bark during training can decrease your dog's desire to bark at other times. It is important to mark and reward your dog after they bark one time during this exercise. This way you are only reinforcing one bark when you cue them to Speak, preventing them from learning to bark continuously. I highly suggest that you teach your dog Quiet (see page 113), too!

How Long Will It Take? 10 repetitions two times per day for three weeks for each visual and verbal cue

1. Use a treat, toy, or ball to get your dog to play tug or fetch.

2. Once your dog is interested in the toy, hold it high above their head and out of reach.

3. Once your dog is engaged and clearly desires the item, ask them for a Sit and hold the item above their head. If they jump, pull the toy away. You may have to wait for a bit, but your dog will likely get frustrated and bark.

4. Mark your dog as correct with your clicker or marker word the moment your dog barks.

5. Reward with a treat. Be sure to only reward for one bark.

NEED HELP?

Be patient when working on this trick. You may need to try over a few days to capture only one bark and reinforce it correctly.

HOW TO ADD A VISUAL CUE

1. Remove the toy and hold your hand in a duckbill shape. Open and close your hand slowly once or twice.

2. Wait for your dog to bark and then mark as correct when they bark one time.

3. Reward with a treat.

HOW TO ADD A VERBAL CUE

1. Say the verbal cue "Speak" one time just before showing the visual cue to your dog.

2. Mark when your dog barks once.

3. Reward with a treat.

4. When your dog begins to respond to the verbal cue consistently, start to add a pause after you say the verbal cue to give your dog time to offer the correct behavior.

5. When your dog begins to respond consistently to the cues, you can pick either the verbal or visual cue to ask them to Speak.

Difficulty Level: Intermediate

Verbal Cue
Quiet

Visual Cue
Finger to lips as if
saying "Shh"

Required Tricks
Sit, Speak

Does your dog love to bark? If so, you will love this trick, which teaches you how to get them to be silent instantly. It is important that you do not over-use this cue too much at the beginning or under reinforce it as you want it to be a trick that is always highly rewarded. Always highly reinforce your dog for being quiet with special treats. As you use your clicker or marker word, think of trying to capture the moment of silence.

How Long Will It Take? 10 repetitions two times per day for five weeks for each visual and verbal cue

TRY THIS

1. Cue your dog to Sit in front of you.

2. Cue your dog to Speak.

3. When your dog barks, put your finger to your lips and wait for a moment of silence.

4. Mark the moment of silence as correct with your clicker or marker word.

5. Reward your dog with a treat two or three times while they sit quietly.

NEED HELP?

As your dog starts to understand this cue, you will be able to extend the period of silence. Try to always mark and reward before your dog becomes frustrated, which may cause them to bark. Doing so will allow you to build the behavior up successfully and will prevent you from encouraging more barking.

Vary the time between treats so that your dog isn't able to predict the time interval.

HOW TO ADD A VERBAL CUE

1. Cue your dog to Sit in front of you.

2. Cue your dog to Speak.

3. After they bark, say the verbal cue "Quiet" one time and then put your finger to your lips.

4. Mark the moment of silence as correct.

5. Reward with a treat.

6. When your dog begins to respond to the verbal cue consistently, start to add a pause after you say the verbal cue to give your dog time to offer the correct behavior.

7. When your dog begins to respond consistently to the cues, you can pick either the verbal or visual cue to ask them for Quiet.

8. Gradually begin to increase the amount of time that they must stay silent. Start with one second and build up to 10 or more seconds.

Balance a Treat

Difficulty Level: Intermediate

Verbal Cues
Down, Stay,
Leave It

Visual Cue
None

Required Tricks
Down, Stay, Leave It

Balancing a treat is a clever trick and is always an entertaining one to work on. It teaches your dog how to balance a treat and leave it on their paws and nose until you release them to eat it. This is a great advanced impulse control exercise, which helps your dog learn to work through frustration. Remember to reward for each small step in the right direction.

How Long Will It Take? 10 repetitions two times per day for four weeks for each visual and verbal cue

1. Cue your dog into a Down and Stay and place a treat on the floor.

2. Cue your dog to leave the treat with Leave It.

3. Mark your dog correct with a clicker or marker word if they leave the treat.

4. Reward your dog with the treat by saying "Okay" to release them.

5. Start to move the treat closer to one paw. If they move their mouth toward the treat, take it away. If they stay still, mark and reward.

6. Try to get the treat to touch your dog's paw. Then try for both paws.

7. Mark your dog correct with a clicker or marker word when they "Leave It."

8. Reward by releasing them with "Okay" to get the treat(s).

1. Cue your dog into a Down and Stay and place a treat on the floor.

2. Cue your dog to leave the treat with Leave It.

3. Start to move the treat closer to the top of their snout. If they move their head, take the treat away. If your dog stays still, mark and reward.

4. Work in small steps until you can get the treat to touch your dog's nose. Then try to work up to balancing the treat on their nose.

5. Mark your dog as correct with your clicker or marker word the moment the treat touches the top of their nose.

6. Build up to taking your hand off the treat.

7. Reward by releasing them with "Okay" to get the treat.

NEED HELP?

As your dog learns this trick, reward any moment you can move the treat. closer to their nose or paw without your dog trying to get it.

Hide and Go Seek

Difficulty Level: Intermediate

Verbal Cue
Find Me

Visual Cue
None

Required Tricks
Sit, Stay

If you like playing games with your dog, you'll enjoy this trick. Hide and Go Seek teaches your dog to Stay while you hide and then they find you on your cue. This trick makes a fun activity for the whole family. Be sure to review Stay (see page 41) before starting this trick. Hide in easy spots at first, then work up to harder spots.

How Long Will It Take? 10 repetitions two times per day for four weeks for each visual and verbal cue

1. Cue your dog into a Sit and Stay.

2. Walk out of your dog's sight line and hide nearby.

3. Release your dog to come find you by saying, "Okay, find me."

4. Make a noise like a kissy sound or a clap to help your dog find you the first few times, then fade this out.

5. Mark your dog as correct with a clicker or marker word when they find you.

6. Reward with a treat or toy.

NEED HELP?

Ask for "Stay" on a bed or blanket. This gives your dog a specific surface and defined boundaries to practice staying. If your dog is getting up frequently, you will need to review a "Sit Stay" from chapter 3 (see page 42).

Clean Up: Put Your Toys Away

Difficulty Level: Advanced

Verbal Cue
Clean Up

Visual Cue
Pointing to a toy
with verbal cue
"Clean Up"

Required Tricks
Fetch, Get It, Drop It

Tired of picking up after your pet? Train your dog to clean up after themselves with this entertaining and handy skill. After your dog has been playing, ask them to put their toys away on cue. This trick will save you time and will "wow" anyone you show it to. It will take a lot of repetition for your dog to master this trick. You can use a bin, basket, drawer, bucket, cardboard box, or any other type of container to train this trick.

How Long Will It Take? 10 repetitions two times per day for eight weeks for each visual and verbal cue

1. Start by playing Fetch with your dog with one of their favorite toys. After your dog grabs on to the toy with their mouth, encourage them to come back to you and Drop It into your hands.

2. Mark your dog as correct with your clicker or marker word when they drop the toy into your hands.

3. Reward by throwing the toy or playing tug.

1. Take out a bin or a box and set it next to you.

2. Throw a toy for your dog to Fetch and encourage them to bring it back to you.

3. As your dog approaches you with the toy, hold your hands over the bin and cue them to Drop It. Move your hands apart as your dog drops the toy so that it falls into the bin.

4. Mark your dog as correct with your clicker or marker word when the toy drops into the bin.

5. Reward by playing fetch or tug with your dog.

6. Try this with two or three more toys.

1. Arrange a few toys in a pile.

2. Cue your dog to Get It while pointing to the pile of toys. You may need to pick one toy up and move it to encourage your dog to put their mouth on the toy.

3. Cue your dog to walk to the box with the toy by pointing toward it.

4. When your dog drops the toy in the box, immediately cue them to grab another toy by pointing at the pile or picking one up and moving it around.

5. Repeat until all of the toys are in the box, then mark your dog as correct with your clicker or marker word.

6. Reward your dog with a treat or play time.

NEED HELP?

Have your dog put one toy away first. Make sure they understand the cue before adding more toys.

Keep the toy near the box until your dog understands the behavior, then you can add distance.

HOW TO ADD A VERBAL CUE

1. Scatter toys farther apart from each other.

2. Say the verbal cue "Clean Up" one time just before the "Get It" cue and point to the pile of toys.

3. Encourage your dog to pick up any toy and bring it to the box, and cue them to Drop It in.

4. Immediately cue your dog to grab another toy and repeat until all of the toys are in the bin.

5. As your dog becomes more confident with this trick, take out all of the cues other than the verbal cue "Clean Up".

Difficulty Level: Advanced

Verbal Cue
Get Your Leash

Visual Cue
Point to leash

Required Tricks
Get It, Leave It,
Fetch, Drop It

When you get ready to take your dog out for a walk, ask them to assist by grabbing their leash and bringing it to you. This is an adorable trick that you can use on walks as well. If your dog is allowed to go off-leash on a hike, you can ask them to carry their leash for you. This trick will take a bit of time and patience but the work is worth it.

How Long Will It Take? 10 repetitions two times per day for five weeks for each visual and verbal cue

TRY THIS (PHASE 1)

1. With the leash unattached to your dog, hold it in your hand and fold it three or four times.

2. Cue your dog to put their mouth on the leash by using the "Get It" cue.

3. Mark your dog as correct using a clicker or marker word to mark the moment that they grab onto the leash with their mouth.

4. Cue your dog to Drop It in your hands.

5. Mark your dog as correct with your clicker or marker word when they drop the leash in your hands.

6. Reward with a treat.

TRY THIS (PHASE 2)

1. Set your dog's leash on the ground and cue them to Leave It.

2. When you are ready to cue your dog to get their leash, say "Okay" to release them. Then cue Get It to encourage them to grab the leash with their mouth.

3. When your dog grabs onto the leash with their mouth, encourage them to come to you and Drop It in your hands.

4. Mark as correct with your clicker or marker word when they drop the leash in your hands.

5. Reward with a treat.

NEED HELP?

Try to play with your dog before asking them to grab onto their leash. Doing so will get them practicing the behavior of grabbing onto something with their mouth and will help them understand what you want them to do with the leash.

HOW TO ADD A VERBAL CUE

1. Set your dog's leash on the ground and cue them to Leave It.

2. When you are ready, give the verbal cue, "Okay, Get Your Leash. Get It," one time just before pointing to the leash.

3. Encourage your dog to bring it back to you.

4. Mark as correct when your dog brings the leash and drops it in your hands.

5. As you practice, fade out saying "Get It" so the cue becomes "Get Your Leash."

Treasure Hunt

Difficulty Level: Advanced

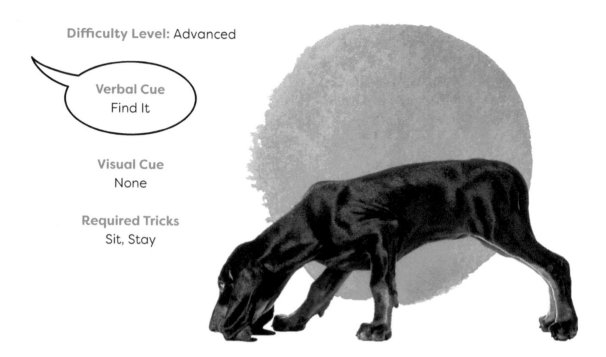

Verbal Cue
Find It

Visual Cue
None

Required Tricks
Sit, Stay

Teach your dog to find hidden treats on cue. Using your dog's scent skills taps into a part of their brain that they instinctively love to use. In this trick, you will hide treats while your dog is in a Stay, then you'll release them to go look. This can be a really great activity to play with kids. Be sure to practice with easy hiding spots while your dog is learning this trick.

How Long Will It Take? 10 repetitions two times per day for four weeks for each visual and verbal cue

1. Start by cueing your dog to Sit and Stay.

2. Take two steps back, cue your dog to Leave It, and set a treat on the ground.

3. Say, "Okay, Find It," and then mark your dog as correct with your clicker or marker word the moment they find the treat.

4. Reward with the treat that was hidden.

5. Cue your dog to Sit and Stay and then go out of their view and hide a treat. Start with an easy spot.

6. When the treat is hidden, release your dog to the treat by using the release word "Okay. Find It."

7. Mark your dog as correct with your clicker or marker word the moment they find the treat.

NEED HELP?

Practice Leave It and Stay if your dog keeps moving from the spot you want them to Stay in.

Cue your dog to Stay on a blanket, mat, or towel.

If they are having trouble finding the treat, you can show them where it is.

Mark and reward any decision to sniff around until they enjoy searching more.

HOW TO ADD A VERBAL CUE

1. Cue your dog to Sit and Stay. Walk away and place the treat in a secret spot.

2. When you are ready, say, "Okay, Find It," to cue your dog to search for the treat.

3. Mark your dog as correct and reward when they find the treat.

Nod Yes

Difficulty Level: Advanced

Verbal Cue
Nod

Verbal Cue
Nod

Visual Cue
Nod your head

Required Tricks
Down

Get your dog talking by teaching them to nod their head yes. This trick will take precise timing and persistence to learn. Move slowly when you lure your dog's head. Try to capture the moment they complete a nod. Once your dog knows this cue, you can teach them to answer any question with a "yes" answer on cue.

How Long Will It Take? 10 repetitions two times per day for two weeks for each visual and verbal cue

1. Cue your dog into a Down.

2. Hold a treat in a closed fist near your dog's nose. Slowly move the treat an inch or two down and back up to where you started, which will cause your dog's head to make a nodding motion.

3. Mark your dog as correct with your clicker or marker word when they follow your lure and make a nodding motion with their head.

4. Reward with a treat.

1. Take the treat out of your cue hand and cue your dog to nod by moving your fist up and down.

2. Mark your dog as correct with your clicker or marker word when they nod and reward from your other hand.

3. Slowly begin to change the visual cue into a small motion of your fist moving up and down.

At first, you can reward any time your dog moves their head. Once they get the idea that you are rewarding for their head moving, you can start to shape the nod how you would like it.

1. Hold your hand near your face and nod your head while you lure.

2. Mark when your dog Nods.

3. Reward with a treat.

4. Slowly phase out the hand motion, until you are only nodding your head to cue. When your dog begins to respond to the visual cue consistently, start to add a pause after you show your dog the visual cue to give them time to offer the correct behavior.

5. Mark your dog as correct when your dog Nods, and reward with a treat.

HOW TO ADD A VERBAL CUE

1. Say the verbal cue "Nod" one time just before showing the visual cue to your dog.

2. Mark when your dog Nods.

3. Reward with a treat.

4. When your dog begins to respond to the verbal cue consistently, start to add a pause after you say the verbal cue to give your dog time to offer the correct behavior.

5. When your dog begins to respond consistently to the cues, you can pick either the verbal or visual cue to ask them for a Nod.

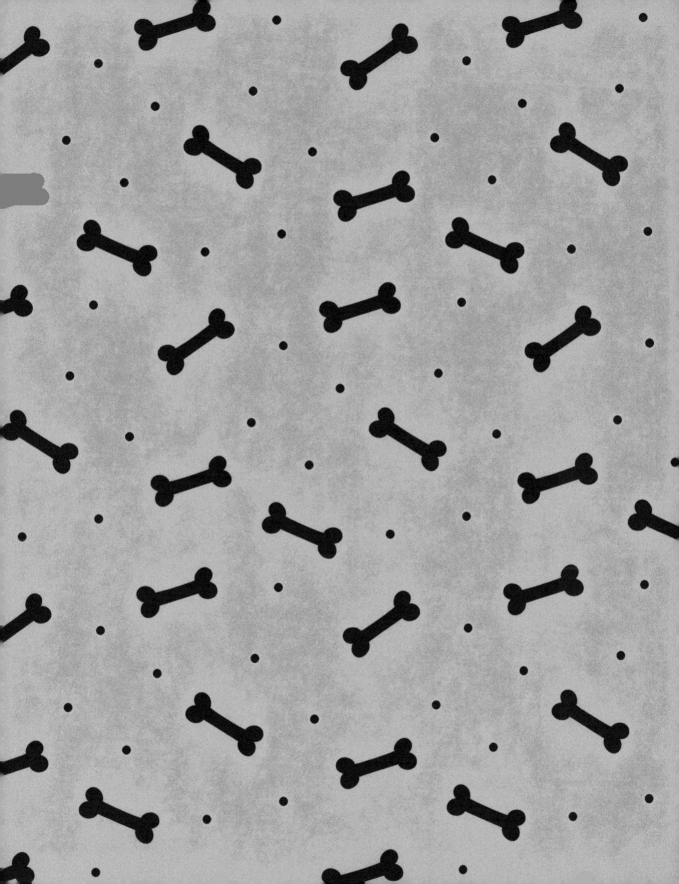

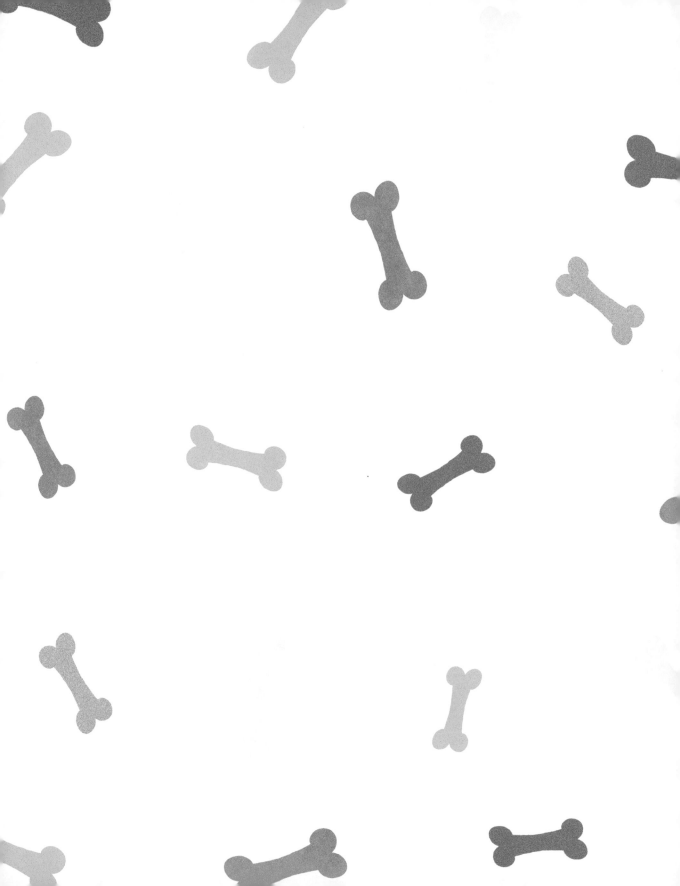

CHAPTER 7

Put on a Show

Turn your dog into a movie star with this set of award-worthy moves. These tricks require dedication and persistence to learn. Many of these moves mimic common human behaviors such as putting your chin down or crossing your legs. By working through this chapter, you'll learn how to train very tiny movements on cue. To train subtle cues, like having your dog lick their lips, you must mark your dog with your clicker or marker word at the exact moment that they are offering you the correct behavior. Treats, Clicker, Action!

Go to Bed

Difficulty Level: Easy

Verbal Cue
Go to Bed

Visual Cue
Point to your
dog's bed

Required Tricks
Down

This can be a helpful cue for times when you want your dog to stay in one spot. Use this cue when you have someone at your front door or when you are cooking in the kitchen and want to keep your dog on their bed. This cue will teach your dog to love their bed. You can also use this trick to calm your pup down.

How Long Will It Take? 10 repetitions two times per day for three weeks for each visual and verbal cue

1. Use a treat to lure your dog onto their bed.

2. Mark your dog as correct with your clicker or marker word when all four paws are on top of the bed.

3. Cue your dog into a Down position on the bed.

4. Mark your dog as correct with your clicker or marker word when they lie down on the bed.

5. Reward with a treat.

NEED HELP?

Practice Up (see page 73) on the object to get your dog comfortable before you add the Down position.

Be sure to add duration and distance separately.

HOW TO WORK THE TREAT OUT OF YOUR CUE HAND

1. Pinch a treat between your thumb and fingertips in both hands.

2. Place your left hand behind your back.

3. Lure your dog onto the bed with your right hand and cue them into the Down position.

4. Mark your dog as correct when they lie down on the bed.

5. Reward with a treat from your left hand.

6. Take the treats out of your right hand. Pretend to have a treat in your right hand and lure onto the bed and cue Down again.

7. Mark when they lie down on the bed and reward from your left hand.

8. Repeat with your left hand giving the cue and your right hand behind your back. Keep practicing until your dog responds consistently when you use an empty cue hand.

HOW TO ADD A VISUAL CUE

1. Start to point to the bed without a treat in your hand.

2. Mark your dog as correct when they go on the bed with all four paws.

3. Cue your dog Down on the bed.

4. Mark your dog as correct when your dog goes into a down position on the bed.

5. Reward with a treat.

6. Release with "Okay" and toss a treat to encourage your dog to get up.

HOW TO ADD A VERBAL CUE

1. Say the verbal cue "Go to Bed" one time just before showing the visual cue to your dog.

2. Mark when your dog lies down on the bed.

3. Reward with a treat.

4. When your dog begins to respond to the verbal cue consistently, start to add a pause after you say the verbal cue to give your dog time to offer the correct behavior.

5. When your dog begins to respond consistently to the cues, you can pick either the verbal or visual cue to ask them to go to bed.

Difficulty Level: Easy

Verbal Cue
Belly Up

Visual Cue
Open palm facing
up, flip over hand
for cue

Required Tricks
Down

In this trick, your dog will roll onto their back for a belly rub. Dog tummies are so adorable and deserve to be seen. Some dogs dislike being on their back. To teach a dog to slowly like this position, use a very high-value treat and reward for really tiny movements over a month or two. If your dog likes belly rubs, they will love this trick.

How Long Will It Take? 10 repetitions two times per day for four weeks for each visual and verbal cue

1. Cue your dog to Down in front of you.

2. Hold the treat close to your dog's nose and then slowly curve the treat toward one of your dog's shoulders. When your dog's nose moves toward their shoulder, their weight will shift onto one of their hips, creating a C curve with their body.

3. Let your dog nibble or lick at the treat and slowly bring it across your dog's shoulder line, which will cause them to roll onto their back with their belly up.

4. Mark your dog as correct with your clicker or marker word when they roll onto their back.

5. Continue to reward as your dog holds this position.

6. Release them with "Okay" and reward with a treat.

NEED HELP?

If your dog knows Roll Over, you will need to slow them down as you start to roll them over in order to prevent them from rolling over to the opposite side.

Let your dog nibble at the treat as you slowly lure them.

HOW TO WORK THE TREAT OUT OF YOUR CUE HAND

1. Pinch a treat between your thumb and fingertips in both hands.

2. Place your left hand behind your back.

3. Cue your dog to Down in front of you. Lure your dog onto their back with your right hand.

4. Mark your dog as correct when they are on their back.

5. Reward with a treat from your left hand.

6. Take the treats out of your right hand. Pretend to have a treat in your right hand and ask for Belly Up again.

7. Mark when they Belly Up and reward from your left hand.

8. Repeat with your left hand giving the cue and your right hand behind your back. Keep practicing until your dog responds consistently when you use an empty cue hand.

HOW TO ADD A VISUAL CUE

1. Cue your dog into a Down position.

2. Lure them into Roll Over by bringing your hand close to your dog's nose with your palm flat and facing up. Bring your hand from their nose to their shoulder and then flip your hand as you gesture over their body, cueing them to roll onto their back.

3. Mark when your dog rolls onto their back.

4. Reward with a treat.

5. As you practice, gradually stand straight up and transition the hand signal to be a quick flip of the hand.

6. Mark your dog as correct when your dog Rolls Over and reward with a treat.

HOW TO ADD A VERBAL CUE

1. Say the verbal cue "Belly Up" one time just before showing the visual cue to your dog.

2. Mark when your dog rolls onto their back.

3. Reward with a treat.

4. When your dog begins to respond to the verbal cue consistently, start to add a pause after you say the verbal cue to give your dog time to offer the correct behavior.

5. When your dog begins to respond consistently to the cues, you can pick either the verbal or visual cue to ask them for a Belly Up.

Who's Your Best Friend?

Difficulty Level: Intermediate

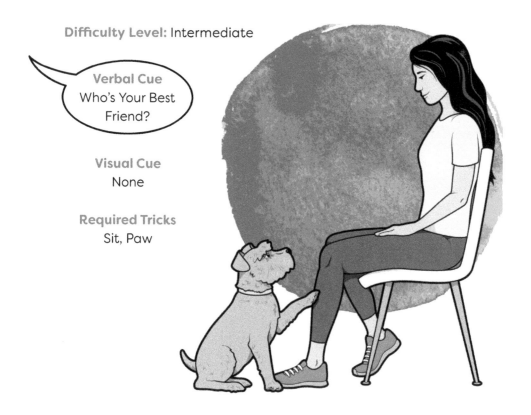

Verbal Cue
Who's Your Best Friend?

Visual Cue
None

Required Tricks
Sit, Paw

Crack up your audience with this trick, which cues your dog to put their paw on you when you ask the question, "Who's your best friend?" This joyous trick will always make you feel special. You will adore using this cue and find that it always makes people smile.

How Long Will It Take? 10 repetitions two times per day for four weeks for each visual and verbal cue

1. Sit in a chair or on the floor and cue your dog to Sit in front of you.

2. Warm up your dog with several repetitions of Paw.

3. Put your hand near your knee or mid-shin and cue Paw.

4. Mark your dog correct with your clicker or marker word when their paw touches your hand.

5. Reward with a treat.

NEED HELP?

Try three repetitions using your hand as the cue to Paw and then one repetition where you still use the verbal cue, but offer your leg for your dog to paw as the visual cue.

HOW TO ADD A VERBAL CUE

1. Add the verbal cue "Friend" just before you put your hand on your leg.

2. Mark your dog correct when they touch their paw to your hand.

3. Reward with a treat.

4. Remove your hand and say the verbal cue "Friend." Look toward your leg to help your dog understand where to target with their paw.

5. Mark your dog as correct when they touch their paw to your leg.

6. Reward with a treat.

7. Stand up and hold your knee out so that it is slightly bent.

8. Cue your dog to Paw your leg using the verbal cue "Who's Your Best Friend?"

9. Mark your dog as correct when they touch their paw to your leg.

10. Reward with a treat.

11. Work to stand up straight and cue your dog to paw at you with the cue "Who's Your Best Friend?"

Are You Tired? (Chin Down)

Difficulty Level: Intermediate

Verbal Cue
Are You Tired?

Visual Cue
Touch the back
of your fingers to
your chin

Required Tricks
Down

Cue your dog to rest their chin on the floor. To get a laugh, you can use the verbal cue "Are You Tired?" This cue can be used when you want your dog to relax. Similar to the way your dog's nose touches your hand for Touch (see page 25), their chin will target the floor.

How Long Will It Take? 10 repetitions two times per day for four weeks for each visual and verbal cue

1. Cue your dog Down on the floor.

2. Hold a treat that your dog really loves in your right hand in a fist.

3. Hold your hand near your dog's nose.

4. Slowly move the treat downward to gently lure your dog's head toward the ground. Keep your dog's neck in line with their spine to encourage them to touch their chin to the floor.

5. When your dog's chin touches the floor, mark your dog as correct with your clicker or marker word.

6. Reward with a treat.

NEED HELP?

Try using a towel or blanket so your dog can feel the texture when their chin touches it.

To add duration, reward your dog while they have their chin on the ground. Quickly take the treat away and bring it back if they keep their chin touching the floor. Start with rapid repetitions and slowly add more time between treats.

HOW TO WORK THE TREAT OUT OF YOUR CUE HAND

1. Hold a treat in both of your fists.

2. Place your left hand behind your back.

3. Cue your dog Down on the floor, then lure your dog to touch their chin to the floor with your right hand.

4. Mark your dog as correct when their chin touches the floor.

5. Reward with a treat from your left hand.

6. Take the treats out of your right hand. Pretend to have a treat in your right hand, cue Down, and lure your dog's chin to the floor again.

7. Mark when they rest their chin on the floor and reward from your left hand.

8. Repeat with your left hand giving the cue and your right hand behind your back. Keep practicing until your dog responds consistently when you use an empty cue hand.

HOW TO ADD A VISUAL CUE

1. Cue your dog Down. Touch the back of your fingers to your chin, then lure them into the resting position using a treat to remind them of the behavior.

2. Mark when your dog rests their chin on the floor.

3. Reward with a treat.

4. When your dog begins to respond to the visual cue consistently, start to add a pause after you show your dog the visual cue to give them time to offer the correct behavior.

5. Mark your dog as correct when your dog rests their chin on the floor and reward with a treat.

HOW TO ADD A VERBAL CUE

1. Say the verbal cue "Are You Tired?" one time just before showing the visual cue to your dog.

2. Mark when your dog rests their chin on the ground.

3. Reward with a treat.

4. When your dog begins to respond to the verbal cue consistently, start to add a pause after you say the verbal cue to give your dog time to offer the correct behavior.

5. When your dog begins to respond consistently to the cues, you can pick either the verbal or visual cue to ask them for an Are You Tired?

How Was Your Dinner? (Lick Your Lips)

Difficulty Level: Intermediate

Verbal Cue
How Was Your Dinner?

Visual Cue
None

Required Tricks
Sit

Cue your dog to give compliments to the chef by teaching them to lick their lips on cue. This is a silly, endearing trick to ask for after your pup has had their dinner, showing how much they enjoyed their meal.

How Long Will It Take? 10 repetitions two times per day for six weeks for each visual and verbal cue

TRY THIS

1. Cue your dog to Sit in front of you and give your dog a few nibbles of the treat in your hand.

2. Pull your hand away and back up near your collarbone.

3. Your dog is likely to lick at their lips after swallowing the bit of treat they just ate. This is especially true with foods like peanut butter, cream cheese, or other dog-safe soft spreads.

4. Mark your dog as correct with your clicker or marker word at the exact moment they lick their lips.

5. Reward with a treat.

NEED HELP?

The timing of your clicker or marker word must be extremely precise. Mark the exact moment that your dog licks their lips. This is such a subtle behavior that it takes a lot of precision and practice to get this trick down.

HOW TO ADD A VERBAL CUE

1. Give your dog a nibble or lick of a treat.

2. Pull the treat back and quickly say the verbal cue "Dinner."

3. Mark your dog as correct when they lick their lips.

4. Reward with a treat.

5. Add the rest of the verbal cue "How Was Your Dinner?" to cue your dog to lick their lips after you give them a bite of a treat.

6. Mark your dog as correct when they lick their lips.

7. Reward with a treat.

8. Say the verbal cue "How Was Your Dinner?" and pause. Wait to see if your dog will lick their lips.

9. Mark and reward when they lick their lips.

Difficulty Level: Advanced

Verbal Cue
Cross Your Paws

Visual Cue
None

Required Tricks
Down, Paw

Looking to get your dog on the cover of a magazine? Teach them to cross their paws and they will be ready for a fashion shoot. You will use your foundation work on Paw (see page 27) when learning this cue. This trick will take time and precision. Be really patient with your dog and remember that they are trying their best to understand you. Move slowly and mark precisely.

How Long Will It Take? 10 repetitions two times per day for eight weeks for verbal cue

1. Cue your dog to offer a Down in front of you and then ask for their paw. Practice this step until your dog can consistently offer Paw in a Down position.

2. Hold your left hand across from your dog's right shoulder.

3. Move your left hand about two inches to your right. Hand cue your dog to give you their right paw.

4. Mark your dog as correct with your clicker or marker word when they touch their right paw to your hand.

5. Reward with a treat.

6. Continue to move your hand over two inches at a time until your hand is over your dog's left paw when you cue them to offer their paw.

7. Move your hand two more inches, moving to the outside of your dog's left paw.

8. Mark your dog as correct with your clicker or marker word when they paw your hand.

9. Reward with a treat.

10. Bring your hand closer to the floor when you cue them to Paw your hand and then quickly take your hand away so that they cross their paws.

11. Mark as correct when their paws cross.

12. Reward with a treat.

Reward for any movement of the paw in the right direction. Doing so will keep your dog feeling successful and motivated.

HOW TO WORK THE TREAT OUT OF YOUR CUE HAND

1. Pinch a treat between your thumb and fingertips in both hands.

2. Place your left hand behind your back.

3. Cue your dog to Down. Lure your dog to Cross Your Paws with your right hand.

4. If your dog crosses their paws, mark them as correct. If your dog doesn't respond, make a motion from right to left to encourage their paw to move in the right direction. Be patient with this step.

5. Reward with a treat.

6. Take the treats out of your right hand. Pretend to have a treat in your right hand and ask for Cross Your Paws again.

7. Mark when they cross their paws and reward from your left hand.

8. Repeat with your left hand giving the cue and your right hand behind your back. Keep practicing until your dog responds consistently when you use an empty cue hand.

HOW TO ADD A VERBAL CUE

1. Say the verbal cue "Cross Your Paws" one time just before asking for Cross Your Paws.

2. Mark when your dog crosses their paws.

3. Reward with a treat. When your dog begins to respond to the verbal cue consistently, start to add a pause after you say the verbal cue to give your dog time to offer the correct behavior.

Monkey

Difficulty Level: Advanced

> **Verbal Cue**
> Monkey

Visual Cue
Holding forearm up near dog and parallel to the ground with verbal cue "Monkey"

Required Tricks
Sit Pretty

Turn your canine into a primate with this goofy trick, which cues your dog to put their paws on your arm and then poke their head through the gap. This trick is hard physically for your dog and requires that they have some flexibility in their shoulders. Work slowly and don't push your dog too quickly with this trick. If you are patient and shape this trick over a few weeks or even months, you will be able to show off this unique and funny trick.

How Long Will It Take? 10 repetitions two times per day for eight weeks for each visual and verbal cue

1. Cue your dog to Sit Pretty and present your forearm near their shoulders.

2. Encourage their paws to touch your arm by gently moving your arm near your dog's paws.

3. Mark your dog as correct with your clicker or marker word when either paw touches your arm.

4. As your dog gets more comfortable with this, require that they touch both paws to your arm before marking and rewarding.

1. Cue your dog to Sit Pretty and hold your arm out for their paws to touch.

2. Hold a treat just under your forearm, which will encourage your dog's head to move under your arm.

3. Mark your dog as correct with your clicker or marker word for any movement of their head in the direction of the treat.

4. Reward with a treat.

5. Raise your criteria and require that your dog brings their head down and under your forearm, poking their head through the hole.

6. Mark and reward your dog when they poke their head to the other side of the hole.

Work on getting your dog to feel confident with putting their paws on your forearms. Then you can start to slowly shape their head movement by rewarding for every tiny movement the dog's head makes under your arm and between their legs. Some dogs may need to do this while standing on their hind legs instead of on their rear. Try both to see which your dog prefers.

HOW TO WORK THE TREAT OUT OF YOUR CUE HAND

1. Hold a treat in both of your fists.

2. Cue your dog to Sit Pretty with their paws on your forearm.

3. Pretend like you have a treat and lure your dog's head under and through the gap.

4. Mark your dog as correct when they poke their head through.

5. Reward with a treat.

6. Switch hands and repeat.

7. Repeat with your left hand giving the cue and your right hand behind your back. Keep practicing until your dog responds consistently when you use an empty cue hand.

HOW TO ADD A VERBAL CUE

1. Say the verbal cue "Monkey" one time just before presenting your forearm for your dog to rest their paws on.

2. Mark your dog as correct when they offer their head down and under your arm through the hole.

3. Reward with a treat.

4. When your dog begins to respond to the verbal cue consistently, start to add a pause after you say the verbal cue to give your dog time to offer the correct behavior.

Blanket Roll Up

Difficulty Level: Advanced

Verbal Cue
Roll Up

Visual Cue
Pointing to a towel
or blanket with the
verbal cue "Roll Up"

Required Tricks
Grab It, Down,
Roll Over

Train your pup to bundle up in a blanket like a burrito with this fabulous trick. Your dog will lie down, grab onto a blanket or towel with their mouth, and then roll over. The blanket will wrap up around your dog as they roll. The steps in this trick will each take a bit of time to practice, but the results are hilarious. Practice each of the behaviors individually before you chain them together. Make sure your dog can hold the towel or blanket in their mouth for several seconds before attempting to add the Roll Over.

How Long Will It Take? 10 repetitions two times per day for eight weeks for each visual and verbal cue

1. Practice Get It with a blanket or towel. Hold on to the blanket and play with it like a toy to encourage your dog to grab onto it. You must have a solid Get It before moving on.

2. Increase the amount of time your dog is required to hold the blanket in their mouth before you mark with your clicker or marker word and reward them. Start with one second and build up to 10 seconds.

3. Place the blanket on the floor and lure your dog with a treat to walk in the middle and cue Down.

4. Practice this step until your dog offers Down quickly after walking onto the blanket.

5. Cue your dog to grab onto a small bit of the blanket in between their legs. Try holding a treat in your hand with the blanket to encourage your dog to bite it.

6. Mark your dog as correct with your clicker or marker word when they grab the blanket.

7. Reward with a treat.

8. Cue your dog to Roll Over while they are holding onto the blanket with their mouth.

9. Mark your dog as correct with your clicker or marker word when they roll over. As they do so, they will roll up in the blanket.

10. Reward with a treat.

NEED HELP?

You may need to lure your dog several times through each step when adding the verbal cue. Practice frequently and be patient.

HOW TO ADD A VISUAL CUE

1. Take the treats out of your hand and point to the blanket to encourage your dog on to it.

2. Continue to cue "Down," "Grab It," and "Roll Over."

3. Mark your dog as correct when they Roll Over.

4. Reward with a treat.

HOW TO ADD A VERBAL CUE

1. Say "Roll Up" before cueing your dog onto the blanket by pointing at it.

2. Continue to cue "Down," "Grab It," and "Roll Over."

3. Mark your dog as correct when they Roll Over.

4. Reward with a treat.

5. Start to add a pause between the word "Roll Up" and cueing your dog Down to give them time to offer the behavior after hearing the verbal cue.

Point to Owner

Difficulty Level: Advanced

Verbal Cue
Where's Mommy/
Daddy?

Visual Cue
None

Required Tricks
Stand, Paw

This is an extremely clever trick that will teach your dog to point at you with their paw when someone asks them, "Where's Mommy/Daddy?" You will need a lot of repetition to get your dog to understand that they should only point to you when you cue this behavior. Be patient and persistent when learning this trick.

How Long Will It Take? 10 repetitions two times per day for eight weeks

1. Cue your dog to Stand.

2. Cue your dog to Paw in the Stand position.

3. Mark your dog as correct with your clicker or marker word when your dog's paw touches your hand while remaining in Stand.

4. Start with marking your dog after they hold their paw up for one second and gradually increase to rewarding after they hold their paw up for five seconds.

5. Take several steps away and cue your dog to Paw again.

6. Mark your dog as correct with your clicker or marker word when your dog moves their paw.

7. Reward with a treat.

8. Start to shape this behavior by only rewarding the times that they lift their paw up in your direction.

NEED HELP?

Reward for any movement of your dog's paw toward your hand.

Take your hand away quickly when teaching them to lift their leg without targeting your hand.

HOW TO ADD A VERBAL CUE

1. Say the verbal cue "Where's Mommy/Daddy?" and then use the verbal cue "Paw" while your dog is in a Stand position.

2. Mark your dog as correct when they keep their paw up in the air.

3. Reward with a treat.

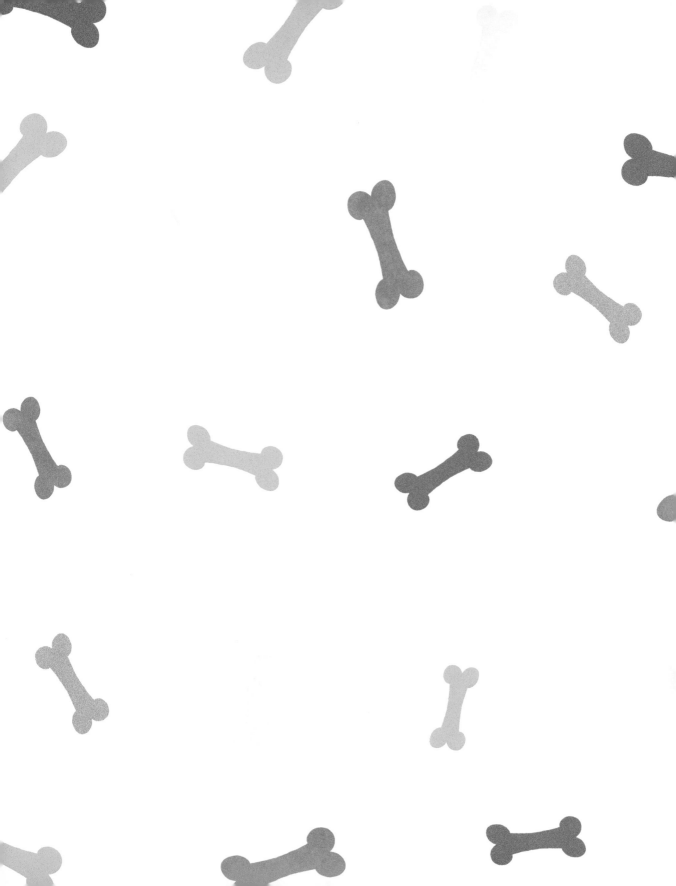

CHAPTER 8

Dance (Canine) Freestyle

Create your own dance routines with your dog after learning the tricks in this chapter. Canine freestyle is a fascinating and surprisingly difficult dog sport in which you train your dog dance routines that the two of you perform to music. Canine freestyle allows you to tap into your creative side with your dog. Many freestyle routines are trained using clicker training and shaping. Remember to mark your dog for the exact moment that they perform the behavior correctly.

Heel

Difficulty Level: Easy

> **Verbal Cue**
> Heel

Visual Cue
Index finger pointing down at side

Required Tricks
Sit, Stand

Learning how to heel is a cue you will need to learn if you want to successfully choreograph and perform canine freestyle. Heel work is also an excellent cue for loose leash walking skills. This exercise works best if you have your dog on leash. The leash keeps your dog close to you and provides a bit of guidance for your dog. Always try to keep the leash hanging loosely in a "J" shape with your hand by your side. The verbal cue "Heel" is used because your dog is positioned near the heel of your foot when walking with you. The ideal position for heeling is your dog walking at your side with their shoulder in line with your leg. At first you will reward frequently, almost every step, but as your dog becomes more familiar with the concept of heeling, you will be able to add more steps between each treat.

How Long Will It Take? 10 repetitions two times per day for eight weeks for both visual and verbal cues

1. With your dog on leash, use a treat near their nose to guide them to a Sit by your left side, facing ahead.

2. Mark your dog as correct with your clicker or marker word when they Sit.

3. Reward with a treat.

4. Take a step forward and immediately mark your dog as correct with your clicker or marker word.

5. Reward your dog by the seam of your pant leg with a treat when your dog keeps their shoulder in line with your leg.

6. Take another step and repeat. Slowly increase the distance between treats.

7. Switch sides and repeat.

NEED HELP?

Hold the treat near your collarbone when you begin training Heel to encourage your dog's gaze to look up at your eyes instead of at your hand.

If your dog pulls ahead, stop and wait for them to reorient toward you. This may be eye contact, walking backward, sitting, etc. It will feel like the leash is getting looser. When they do so, mark and reward.

If your dog doesn't want to move forward, focus on more frequent treating when both of your feet are moving. Try to capture the moments where your dog is moving nicely with you by marking and rewarding.

HOW TO ADD A VISUAL CUE

1. Take the treats out of your hands and point to your right side to encourage your dog to come to your side.

2. Mark your dog as correct when they take a step with you and stay in line with your right leg.

3. Reward with a treat.

4. Repeat on the left side.

HOW TO ADD A VERBAL CUE

1. Point to your right side and say the verbal cue "Heel."

2. Mark your dog as correct when they come to your side. Walk forward and continue to reward by your side as you walk.

3. Reward with a treat. Repeat until they consistently Heel with the verbal cue.

4. Repeat on your left side.

Figure Eight

Difficulty Level: Easy

Verbal Cue
Eight

Visual Cue
Standing with legs apart with one knee slightly bent

Required Tricks
Stand, Heel

Cue your dog to weave through your legs in a figure-eight pattern. This move is enjoyable to teach and fun to perform! Stand with your legs slightly apart. Lean slightly to the left or right to cue your dog to start to go through your legs. You can add this move to any freestyle routine or your daily training regimen.

How Long Will It Take? 10 repetitions two times per day for two weeks for each visual and verbal cue

1. Stand with your dog in front of you with your legs slightly apart.

2. Lean to the right side so that your knee is bent.

3. Bend down and hold the treat behind your leg in the gap between your legs.

4. Move the treat slowly around your leg and to the front to guide your dog.

5. Mark your dog as correct with your clicker or marker word when they complete a circle around one leg.

6. Reward with a treat.

7. Repeat with the other leg.

Once your dog is following the lure, cue them to continue on to the other leg after finishing one leg circle without being rewarded in between.

1. Fade out the lure by pretending like you have a treat in your fist while extending your pointer finger.

2. Use your finger to guide your dog under and around your legs.

3. Mark as correct when they complete the circle around the first leg.

4. Reward with a treat.

5. Repeat circling the other leg.

HOW TO ADD A VERBAL CUE

1. Using a visual cue of slightly bending into your right knee, cue your dog to go through your right and then your left leg.

2. Mark your dog as correct when they circle around both legs.

3. Reward with a treat.

4. Start saying the word "eight" just before you bend your knee.

5. When your dog begins to respond to the verbal cue consistently, start to add a pause after you say the verbal cue to give your dog time to offer the correct behavior.

6. When your dog begins to respond consistently to the cues, you can pick either the verbal or visual cue to ask them for a Figure Eight.

Back Up: Beep, Beep

Difficulty Level: Easy

Verbal Cue
Beep, Beep

Visual Cue
Open, flat palm with fingertips pointing downward, making a pushing motion

Required Tricks
Stand

Learning how to teach your dog to walk backward will build your dog's confidence and body awareness by teaching them to have better hind-end awareness. The footwork for this trick may take your dog a few weeks to learn. You will be able to use this move to create adorable moments in freestyle routines.

How Long Will It Take? 10 repetitions two times per day for six weeks for each visual and verbal cue

1. Cue your dog to Stand in front of you and allow them to nibble at a treat from one of your fists by your side.

2. Slowly move forward toward your dog, which will cause them to take a step backward.

3. Mark your dog as correct with your clicker or marker word for any backward movement they make.

4. Reward with a treat.

5. Repeat and increase the number of steps backward your dog must take before you mark and reward.

NEED HELP?

You may need to push slightly back with your hand that has the treat in it. This will help encourage your dog to move backward.

Reward your dog for any backward movement. This may mean marking and rewarding for even one paw moving back.

HOW TO ADD A VISUAL CUE

1. Take the treats out of your hand and cue your dog to stand in front of you.

2. Step toward them while making a pushing motion with your hand by your side.

3. Mark your dog as correct any time they take a step backward.

4. Reward with a treat.

HOW TO ADD A VERBAL CUE

1. Say the verbal cue "Beep, Beep" one time just before showing the visual cue to your dog.

2. Mark when your dog backs up.

3. Reward with a treat.

4. When your dog begins to respond to the verbal cue consistently, start to add a pause after you say the verbal cue to give your dog time to offer the correct behavior.

5. When your dog begins to respond consistently to the cues, you can pick either the verbal or visual cue to ask them to offer this behavior.

Leg Weaves Walking

Difficulty Level: Intermediate

Verbal Cue
Through

Visual Cue
Stepping with one leg forward and pointing near one side

Required Tricks
Sit

This cue teaches your dog to weave through your legs as you walk forward. After you take a step, your dog goes underneath you and weaves through your legs. Working on this trick is engaging for you and your dog. Be sure to lure your dog toward the leg that is in front.

How Long Will It Take? 10 repetitions two times per day for four weeks for each visual and verbal cue

TRY THIS

1. Stand up and cue your dog to Sit by your left side.

2. Take one step forward with your right foot.

3. Hold a treat in your right hand with your finger pointing down and show it to your dog from the outside of your right leg in the empty space created between your legs.

4. Lure your dog through and mark them as correct with your clicker or marker word when their head is in line with your right foot.

5. Reward with a treat.

6. Take a step forward and repeat on the left side.

NEED HELP?

You will always have your dog on the inside of the leg that is in front and then you will lure your dog from the outside of your front leg to go through.

HOW TO WORK THE TREAT OUT OF YOUR CUE HAND

1. Hold a treat in both of your fists.

2. With your dog on your left side, point your right finger down and show it to your dog from the outside of your right leg in the empty space created between your legs.

3. Mark your dog as correct when they weave through your legs.

4. Reward with a treat from your other hand.

5. Repeat to the other side.

6. Repeat with your left hand giving the cue and your right hand behind your back. Keep practicing until your dog responds consistently when you use an empty cue hand.

1. Stand up and cue your dog to Sit by your left side.

2. Take one step forward with your right foot.

3. With no treats in your hands, point down by your side and show it to your dog from the outside of your right leg in the empty space created between your legs.

4. Mark your dog as correct when their head is in line with your right foot after they cross under your legs.

5. Reward with a treat.

6. Take a step forward and repeat on the left side.

7. As they become more confident, stand up straight and take your pointing fingers away. Take one step, look down, and wait for your dog to go through. If needed, you can remind them with your hand while they are learning.

HOW TO ADD A VERBAL CUE

1. Cue your dog to Sit by your left side.

2. Step forward with your right foot and say the verbal cue "Through" to cue your dog to weave under and through your legs.

3. Mark your dog as correct when they cross all the way to the other side.

4. Reward with a treat.

5. Take a step forward with your left foot and verbally cue your dog to go through to the other side.

6. Mark your dog as correct when they cross all the way to the other side.

7. Reward with a treat.

Dog Circles You

Difficulty Level: Intermediate

Verbal Cue
Circle (R), Loop (L)

Visual Cue
A slight lean to your right and left side

Required Tricks
Stand

This exercise teaches you how to cue your dog to walk in circles around you in both directions. At first, work on getting them to complete one circle before rewarding. As they become more familiar with the behavior you can ask them to continue circling until you cue them to stop. Start with one direction and then teach your dog to go the other way.

How Long Will It Take? At least three weeks for each verbal and visual cue

1. Have your dog stand by your right side and hold a treat in each hand.

2. Use a treat to lure your dog from your right side to your left side by bringing your left hand across the front of your body near your dog's nose.

3. Slowly guide them around to your left side.

4. Mark your dog as correct with your clicker or marker word when your dog is on your left side facing back.

5. Reward with a treat.

6. Continue to lure your dog around your body by guiding your dog with a treat in your left hand around the back of your body over to your right side.

7. Repeat to the opposite side.

NEED HELP?

Try to keep your legs in one spot as you lure your dog around you.

Slowly raise the height of the lure hand until your dog is following the motion of your hand not the treat.

HOW TO WORK THE TREAT OUT OF YOUR CUE HAND

1. Hold a treat in both of your fists.

2. Use a treat to lure your dog from your right side to your left side by bringing your left hand across the front of your body near your dog's nose.

3. Mark your dog as correct when your dog completes a full circle around you.

4. Reward with a treat from your other hand.

5. Repeat to the other side.

6. Pretend to have a treat and lure your dog around you.

7. Mark your dog as correct when they complete a full circle.

8. Reward with a treat.

HOW TO ADD A VISUAL CUE

1. Begin to make the cue more subtle by slightly leaning to the side that you want your dog to start circling.

2. As your dog crosses around, gently lean to the other side to encourage them to complete a full circle.

3. If needed, lure and treat your dog along the way for the first few repetitions.

4. Mark your dog as correct when they complete the circle.

5. Reward with a treat.

HOW TO ADD A VERBAL CUE

1. Starting on the right side, say the verbal cue "Circle" one time just before showing the visual cue to your dog.

2. Mark your dog as correct when your dog completes the circle.

3. Reward with a treat.

4. Switching to the left, say the verbal cue "Loop" one time just before showing the visual cue to your dog.

5. Mark your dog as correct when your dog completes the circle.

6. Reward with a treat.

7. When your dog begins to respond to the verbal cue consistently, start to add a pause after you say the verbal cue to give your dog time to offer the correct behavior.

8. When your dog begins to respond consistently to the cues, you can pick either the verbal or visual cue to ask them to circle you.

Arm Hoop Jumps

Difficulty Level: Intermediate

Verbal Cue
Hoop

Visual Cue
Holding arms out to your side in a ring shape

Required Tricks
Jump Over Arms, Stay

Hold your arms out in a hoop shape and cue your dog to jump through with this acrobatic trick. As a reminder, it is important not to ask your dog to jump too high to prevent injury to their joints. Working at lower heights ensures that your dog can perform a lot of repetitions in good form. I suggest that for dogs under 20 pounds you keep the hoop no higher than two feet off the ground and three feet for dogs over 20 pounds. If you have a puppy or a dog with any sort of physical limitation, keep the hoop close to the ground to protect their joints.

How Long Will It Take? 10 repetitions two times per day for four weeks for each visual and verbal cue

TRY THIS

1. Kneel or sit on the floor. Keep your arm starting from your shoulder to your elbow close to your side and extend your forearm out to the side so that it is parallel to the floor. Cue your dog to jump over your arms.

2. Mark your dog as correct with your clicker or marker word when your dog lands the jump over your arm. If needed, toss a treat to encourage them over.

3. Reward with a treat.

4. Try again while holding your arms starting to form a hoop shape.

NEED HELP?

If your dog is too big to fit through your arms in a hoop shape, hold an imaginary hula hoop to create a circle big enough for your dog. And, if your dog keeps trying to go around the hoop, hold your hoop against a wall so that your dog must go through.

HOW TO ADD A VISUAL CUE

1. Create a hoop with your arms and look to it as a cue, then pause to see if your dog will offer going through. Start kneeling or sitting on the floor, then gradually stand while holding your arms in a hoop.

2. Mark your dog as correct when they are going through the hoop. Toss a treat if needed to remind them.

3. Reward with a treat.

HOW TO ADD A VERBAL CUE

1. Cue your dog to Stay and walk a few steps away.

2. Present your arm hoop and use the verbal cue "Okay, Hoop" to release them to come through the jump.

3. Mark your dog as correct when they are going through the hoop.

4. Reward with a treat.

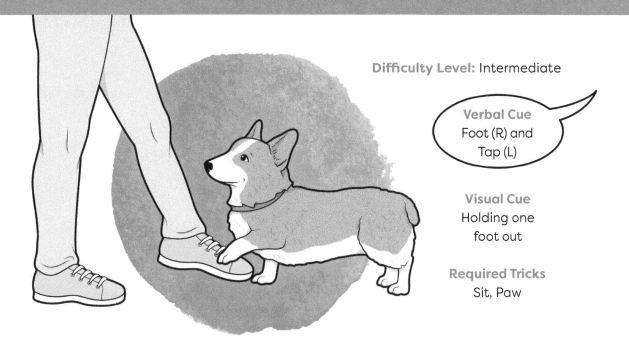

Difficulty Level: Intermediate

Verbal Cue
Foot (R) and
Tap (L)

Visual Cue
Holding one
foot out

Required Tricks
Sit, Paw

Use your feet to cue this clever trick, which teaches your dog to touch their paw to your foot. This trick is helpful in teaching your dog to target their paw to something other than your hand. You can teach your dog to touch any object with their paw or nose if you want to after practicing this concept.

How Long Will It Take? 10 repetitions two times per day for three weeks for each visual and verbal cue

TRY THIS (PHASE 1)

1. Warm your dog up by practicing Paw.

2. Hold a shoe in your hand and hold it out in front of your dog.

3. Cue your dog to Paw while presenting the shoe to them.

4. Mark your dog as correct with your clicker or marker word when they touch their paw to the shoe.

5. Reward with a treat.

TRY THIS (PHASE 2)

1. Put your shoes on your feet and ask your dog to Sit in front of you.

2. Hold out your foot and cue your dog to Paw your foot.

3. When your dog's paw touches your shoe, mark them as correct with your clicker or marker word.

4. Reward with a treat.

NEED HELP?

Work on getting your dog comfortable with touching their paw to your shoe in your hand for several sessions before putting your shoe on your foot.

HOW TO ADD A VERBAL CUE

1. Say the verbal cue "Foot" and present your right foot to your dog.

2. When your dog touches your right foot with their right paw, mark them as correct.

3. Reward with a treat.

4. Say the word "Tap" and present your left foot to your dog.

5. When your dog touches your left foot with their left paw, mark them as correct.

6. Reward with a treat.

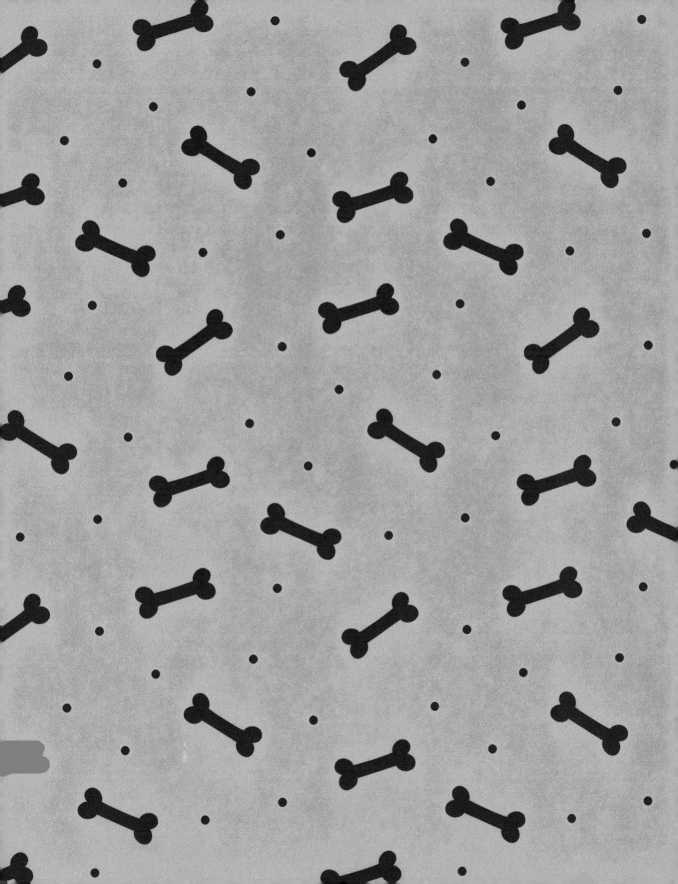

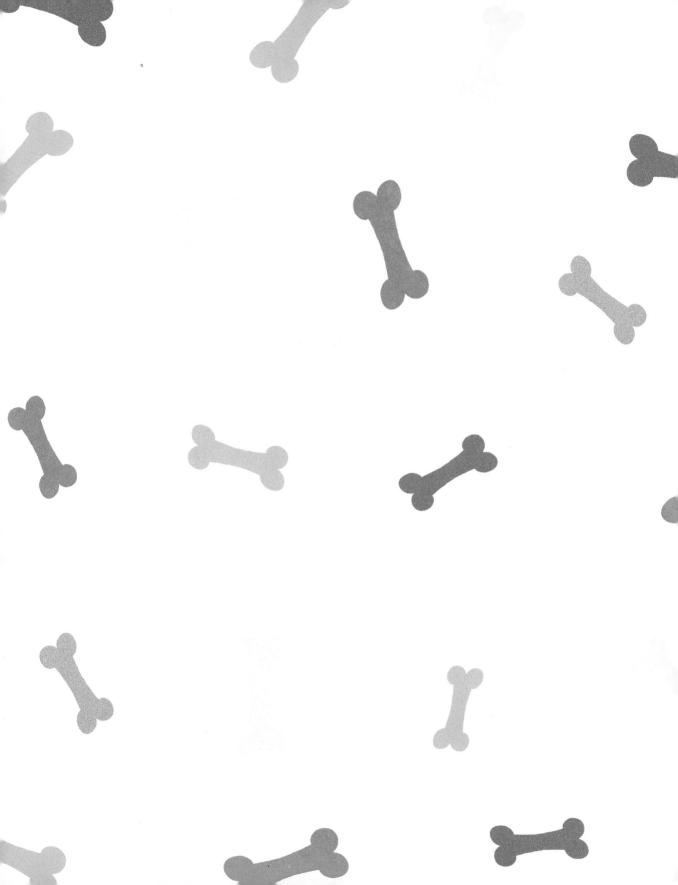

CHAPTER 9

Now You're a Trick Dog!

Congratulations! You and your dog have mastered incredible tricks together! From the basics to learning advanced freestyle behaviors, you have explored a wide variety of tricks in this guide. It's now time to maintain the work you have done through practice. Try to work on every trick in your dog's vocabulary each week to keep the behavior fresh in your dog's mind. If you wish to continue on with more tricks or other dog sports, you will find some resources on the next few pages. Happy training!

Additional Tricks

Now that you have learned the tricks in this book, you can expand your tricks vocabulary with more creative behaviors. There are so many ways to shape and create tricks for your dog. I hope you have learned more about yourself as a teacher and about your dog as a student. Go out there and share all of the hard work you have done!

CHORES	SHOW	AGILITY	CUTE	DANCE	OTHER
Easy:	Easy:	Easy:	Easy:	Easy:	Easy:
Touch Lamp	Hoop	Tunnel	Snuggle	Lift One Leg	Get It Bag
	Jump	Table	Sneeze	Front	Find Person
	Disc	Around	Pose for Camera	Side	
	Catch	Jumps		Back	
		Tire			
Intermediate:	Intermediate:	Intermediate:	Intermediate:	Intermediate:	Intermediate:
Get Newspaper	Bounce Ball (nose)	A-Frame	Sploot	Skip	Green Light, Red Light
Turn On/Off Sink	Jump in Arms	Dog Walk	Curl Up	Pivot	
Get Tissue	Bunny Hop	Roll a Ball	Shake Head No	Chase Your Tail	
Turn On/Off Lights		Wobble Board	Type on Computer	Walk to Side	
		Balance Beam			
Advanced:	Advanced:	Advanced:	Advanced:	Advanced:	Advanced:
Put Trash in Can	Jump in Arms	Weave Poles	I Love You	Cancan	Paint on Canvas
Carry Purse	Handstand	Teeter-Totter	Touch Paws	Prance	Blow Bubbles
Make Bed	Squat	Toss a Toy	Hide Under Blanket	Moonwalk	Play Piano
Clothes to Hamper	Back Stall	Course Work	Move Ears	Twerk	Shake Head No
Get Mail	Foot Stall		Scratch Back	Reverse Circle	Jump Rope
Get a Drink from Fridge	Catch Ring on Nose		Head Tilt	Crawl Backward	Balance on a Ball
Open/Close Drawer	Somersault		Wink	Limp	Growl
			Close Your Eyes	Dance on Hind Legs	Skateboard
			Smile		

Dog Sports and Certifications

If this guide has sparked your interest in other dog sports and activities, I encourage you to explore the resources below. Each dog sport has its own unique qualities and benefits. Spend some time learning about the differences and pick one you think your dog might enjoy to try. Find more information on the American Kennel Club website.

AKC Trick Dog Titles. Through the American Kennel Club (AKC) you can get a certification by having your dog perform a certain set of tricks in front of a certified evaluator. The titles range from novice to elite performer.

Herding. Let your dog tap into their natural instincts with this sport. When your dog is herding, they are expected to move and control livestock in a given area.

Tracking. If your dog is particularly scent driven, tracking may be a perfect activity for you to try. Tracking is when a scent is laid out prior to the dog beginning, and the dog must find different scents. This is great practice for search and rescue pups.

Agility. Running an agility course with your dog is thrilling and fun. A course consists of a set of obstacles that you direct your dog through in a specific order. Dogs compete against each other for the fastest time. I highly recommend trying out agility if you enjoyed working on tricks.

Obedience. Earn a number of titles in obedience, an event where you and your dog follow the instructions of the judge and perform the requested behaviors.

Canine Freestyle. Craft your dance routines with your dog by working on canine freestyle. Freestyle is a fantastic choice for intelligent dogs and creative handlers. Tap into your artistic side and create intricate routines.

Rally. In rally, you and your dog move through a course following the commands that you come across. Teamwork is the goal in this sport. Rally is a great sport for beginning handlers.

Disc Training. Work on your dog's Frisbee skills with disc work. There are a number of activities you can do with your dog and a disc.

RESOURCES

Websites

Andrea Arden Dog Training
www.AndreaArden.com
Karen Pryor Clicker Training
www.clickertraining.com
Dogmantics/Kikopup (Emily Larlham)
www.dogmantics.com
Zak George's Dog Training Revolution
www.dogtrainingrevolution.com
Puppy Culture
www.shoppuppyculture.com

Books

The Other End of the Leash by Patricia McConnell
Don't Shoot the Dog! by Karen Pryor
Dog-Friendly Dog Training by Andrea Arden
How to Behave So Your Dog Behaves by Sophia Yin

Organizations and Associations

American Kennel Club
www.AKC.org
Certification Council for Professional Dog Trainers
www.ccpdt.org
The Association of Professional Dog Trainers
www.apdt.com
International Association of Animal Behavior Consultants
www.iaabc.org

INDEX

ACKNOWLEDGMENTS

Thank you to Andrea Arden for believing in me as a dog trainer and for giving me the opportunity to learn from you. Thank you to Katrina Krings for all you have taught me as a trainer and for always inspiring me with new ideas. Many of the tricks in this book I learned from Katrina, including Monkey, How Was Your Dinner?, Jump Over Legs, and Nod Yes. Thank you to Jo Anne Basinger for getting me hooked on tricks training and for teaching me how to train my dog to do so many tricks. Thank you to the rest of the AADT team for being such wonderful women to work with. To my boyfriend, Turner, thank you for all that you do for me and the dogs. A special thank you to my dogs, Jenga and Rupert, as well as Cooper for being my trick testers. Thanks to my dad and my aunt Roz for your love and support. My love for dogs came from my mom, Enid Richter. This book is dedicated to her.

ABOUT THE AUTHOR

 **Hannah Richter** is a dog trainer and enthusiast based in New York City. After completing an apprenticeship with Andrea Arden Dog Training (AADT), Hannah joined their team and currently teaches classes and private lessons in NYC. She has her CPDT-KA certification and is a member of the Association of Professional Dog Trainers (APDT) and the International Association of Animal Behavior Consultants (IAABC). Hannah is passionate about finding new ways to engage with dogs through positive reinforcement training. She loves to work with dogs on enrichment, including canine fitness, obedience, tricks, and agility. Hannah strives to help dogs and their owners develop deep bonds and strong communication skills using positive reinforcement and management.

Hannah is a proud dog mom to Rupert, a three-year-old silky terrier and Yorkshire terrier mix, and Jenga, a six-month-old mini Australian shepherd. Hannah adores all breeds and has owned a Labrador retriever, a wheaten terrier, a standard poodle, and a Maltipoo.

Hannah is a graduate of Ithaca College's musical theater program. When she is not training dogs, she loves to find opportunities to be creative.

Printed in the USA
CPSIA information can be obtained
at www.ICGtesting.com
LVHW072325101123
763346LV00002B/15